BACK OFF!

The Definitive Guide To Stopping Collection Agency Harassment

Benjamin F. Dover

Equitable Media Services
Fort Worth, Texas

BACK OFF!

*"Adversity reveals genius,
prosperity conceals it."*
Horace

The following company names appear in this book and are registered trademarks of their respective companies: CompUSA, Nickelodeon, fX, TRW, Internet, CompuServe, Maker's Mark, Best Fares Magazine, TransUnion, CSC/Equifax Credit Information Services, VISA, MasterCard, American Express, AMEX, Discover, Chrysler, First USA Bank, First USA Inc., VISA USA, Ford, Radio Shack, Mailboxes, Etc., Western Union, IBM, Computer Sciences Corporation, Mobil, Shell, Sears, Citibank, Chase Manhattan, National Foundation For Consumer Credit, Donahue, The Wall Street Journal, TalkRadio 570/KLIF, Consumer Credit Counseling Service (CCCS), New England Educational Loan Marketing Corporation (Nellie Mae).

U.S. Government publications, Federal Trade Commission, Washington, D.C.: *Facts for Consumers: Fair Credit Reporting*, February 1992; *Credit Repair Scams*, August 1992; Fair Credit Billing, September 1992; Fair Debt Collection, September 1992; *Credit Billing Errors? Use FCBA*, November 1992; *Equal Credit Opportunity*, September 1992; *Public Law 91-508/Title VI, The Fair Credit Reporting Act, as amended by Public Law 95-598*, November 6, 1978; *Commentary on The Fair Credit Reporting Act*, May 1990.

For more information, contact: David Flowers/Media Coordinator, Equitable Media Services, Post Office Box 9822, Fort Worth, Texas 76147-2822.

Library of Congress Cataloging-In-Publication Data:

Dover, Benjamin F.
    Back off! : the definitive guide to stopping collection agency
    harassment / by Benjamin F. Dover ; edited by Jim Donovan.
    p. cm.
    Includes bibliographical references and index.
    Preassigned LCCN: 94-071190
    ISBN 1-880-925-04-4

    1. Collection laws—United States—Popular works. 2. Collection agencies—Law and legislation—United States—Popular works. 3. Consumer credit—Law and legislation—United States—Popular works. I. Donovan, Jim, 1954- II. Title.

KF1024.Z9D69 1994	346.73'077
States. I. Title.	
HG3751.7.D68 1993	332.743
QBI94-890	

This book is available at a special discount when ordering in bulk quantities. For more information, contact:

Equitable Media Services
ATTN: Bulk Sales Department
Post Office Box 9822
Fort Worth, TX 76147-2822

E-mail Benjamin Dover at *CompuServe* address: 75053,3635 or on the *Internet* at: bendover@onramp.net

ACKNOWLEDGEMENTS

Thank you to all of my friends, family and associates who have been a part of my journey. Your support and input have been an invaluable ingredient in my own survival over the years.

Phil Bechtel	Mary & Liberty DeVitto	Katy Gray
Buck & Betty Beneze	John Watson	Stan David
Stan & Cynthia Talley	Bill & Molly	Sharon Hallberg
Scott & Wendy	Kevin & Murphy	Jerry Helper
Homer & Julie	Larry J.	L.G. Reese, III
Bobi Heath	Lora Cain	Norman Higgins
Marshall Day	Bill & Sue Roffey	Ed, Kyle & Mike
Andy Phillips	Wanda S.	Lezlie Fowlkes
Marsha Friedman	Martha Savelo	Floyd Lawson
Dad, Mom & Jim	Angel Martin	Linda & Stacy
Ann Marie Petitto	Eddie Haskell	Jake McCandle
Marti Pounder	Gil Gross	D.M.L. Roberts
Britt Reid	John Broude	Max and Grace
Mike Becker	Susan Kaplow	Dr. Zachary Smith
Hank Kimball	Bretta, Kent & George	Gordon V.
James Rockford	Donna Willard	Will Robinson
Norm Peterson	Ethan B.	Ray Kinsella
Mitch McDeere	R.A. Cruson	Pablo Peebles
Steven Gardner	Duke Slater	Bob Ray Sanders
Linda Vanderwold	Tony Lawrence	Sharon Hallberg
Art Zobal	Gregg Cockrell	Jean N.
Ralph Marshburn	Garry McKinney	Martina O'Boyle

Tom Carter and Debbie Spears, Federal Trade Commission/Dallas office.
Leo Kornfeld, U.S. Department of Education.
C.S. Jenkins, Director of MIS security.
Dan Bennett, Dan Halyburton, John Shomby and the rest of the KLIF staff.
Most of all, I still thank God for a second chance.

Cover design by Rick Sales.
Back cover photo by Photomedia.
Leslie Higgins Advertising of Fort Worth, Texas for their book design expertise.
Tom Parsons & Best Fares Magazine are the official travel coordinators for B.F. Dover and staff
Thank you Nickelodeon and fX for continued inspiration...and my good friends at Austin Nichols and Maker's Mark!
BACK OFF! was written on a Compudyne 486/55 system from CompUSA using WordPerfect software.
8.0 is the official deal-making lunch destination of Benjamin Dover and staff.

WARNING!

You **MUST** read this book at least twice before enacting any of the strategies or tactics that are outlined.

You are about to challenge an incredibly intimidating system that feeds on fear and ignorance of the laws of the land. Without the insights you are about to gain you will be fighting an uphill battle you're destined to lose. The system is stacked against you.

This book may upset many people in a variety of industries across this nation.

Too bad. If empowering the consumer with knowledge of federal laws designed to protect them is what they're accusing me of doing, then so be it.

Ask questions! Challenge the status quo! Don't feel like you deserve the abuse you may already be encountering from the underworld of the debt collection industry. The key now is getting back on your feet and settling up with all of your creditors . . . never the debt collectors!

This book is the nightmare of the debt collection industry because it empowers you, the American consumer, to regain control of your life by showing you how to tell them all to . . .

BACK OFF!

Benjamin F. Dover
Fort Worth, TX
October 1994

DISCLAIMER

I am <u>not</u> an attorney and do not give legal advice.

I am <u>not</u> a certified public accountant and do <u>not</u> give accounting or tax advice.

As with all books published in the Consumer/Self Help genre, it is important that you understand <u>all</u> the information explained in this book **before** proceeding.

This book is <u>not</u> designed to be a guaranteed solution if you are buried under a mountain of debt. In some instances, bankruptcy is a reasonable response to your particular situation. These cases are extreme, and if warranted, I urge you to seek the assistance of a qualified, board-certified bankruptcy attorney. Don't try to solve all of your problems by utilizing this $14.95 solution. It's like trying to cure brain cancer with two aspirin and plenty of rest.

Don't be penny wise and pound foolish. Spend the money where and when it is warranted to get an expert opinion.

Good luck.

FOREWORD

BACK OFF! will work for you—but you must be willing to invest:

TIME
PATIENCE
PERSISTENCE
KNOWLEDGE

The last element is here in this book, but you've got to supply the first three. A few points I'd like to make at the outset:

1) The information and the presentation in this book originate from several areas:

   a) The author's own real-life experiences;

   b) The author's past dealings with individuals having problems described in this book; and

   c) Intensive research by the author, including interviews with recognized experts in the world of debt collection.

2) Some of the people mentioned above spoke on the record. Others cooperated with the understanding that their identities would be concealed because of their current or past association or involvement in the credit/information and debt collection industries.

3) You may be told that this book is little more than a ticket to financial disaster. Yeah, right. Anybody who says that probably has an interest in one of your debts.

BACK OFF! is an incisive and revealing examination of the debt collection industry, and how it systematically abuses consumers across the United States of America as of October 1994.

If you've got your credit cards charged to their limits, you don't need me to help you on your way towards financial ruin. You're already well on your way. What I'm going to do in this book is guide you through the storm and get you back home safely.

4) You may be told I am "abusing the system."
Wrong . . . but why don't you be the judge?

The fact is that millions of honest consumers across America are sick to death of being abused by the system. The debt collection industry routinely crosses the line and abuses federal laws designed to protect consumers. If they utilized more civilized and realistic techniques in collecting past-due debts, they wouldn't continue to be the leading source of complaints to the authorities empowered with enforcing these consumer protection laws on both a state and federal basis.

5) Big banks, department stores and other lenders will publicly dispute everything I'm about to share with you for several reasons:

    a) "Company policy";

    b) "Benjamin Dover is a quick-buck artist selling snake oil";

    c) "It'll never happen like he tells you in his book, so pay up or we'll screw up your credit reports";

    d) "It'll never happen as he tells you in the book so pay up or we'll see you in court";

    e) "Tell that to the police when we send them over to pick you up while you're at work."

Believe them if you wish and take this book back to wherever you bought it **now** so you can get your money back. It's your decision, and I'm not about to force anyone to listen to something they don't want to.

7) This is why they're intimidated by my philosophies:

    a) I have their number and share it with you, the consumer;

    b) I show you how the system works so you won't be intimidated by their strong-arm mail and telephone techniques;

    c) I take away their "hammer" and with it their ability to scare, intimidate and coerce you into doing things that are usually only in their best financial interest, *NOT YOURS.*

Some parting thoughts . . .

As I have already said once before (but it warrants repeating), this book is **not** a blueprint on how to evade debts and responsibilities that you rightly owe. It is a tool to teach you how the system works and to give you the knowledge and insights necessary to get back on your feet emotionally and financially.

But it is not a Band-Aid approach to solving your financial problems. You can't fix something unless you know how it got broken. Your financial situation didn't deteriorate overnight—so don't think that you're going to fix it overnight either.

The methods used in *BACK OFF!* weren't learned from any one source or person but (unfortunately) from **trial by fire** . . . and also from a substantial amount of time studying the system.

You will see immediate results in your own life as you **regain control** of your situation.

Will you successfully stop third-party debt collector harassment 100% of the time?

Absolutely! No question. If you implement the plan in this book, it really **will** work!

People in a variety of socio-economic groups have benefitted from the knowledge you are about to gain, including truck drivers, school teachers, nurses and doctors and dentists, radio and television personalities, real estate developers and bankers . . . and (believe it or not) even a few attorneys.

I've seen the highs and lows of the Texas economy of the 1980s, and the difficult economic times being endured by people just like you in professions as diverse as the automobile industry, oil and gas, defense contractors, and even "stable" careers with industry giants like IBM. **Nobody** is safe from the ax of unemployment or from the upheaval of an unhappy marriage, from the death of a loved one or an unexpected illness or accident.

We just can't seem to plan for the troubled times we're all forced to face at some point in our lives . . . and you never know what to expect or how to react until you're suddenly forced into the midst of your own personal hell.

To those individuals who intentionally abuse the system and rip off creditors big and small and who think they are beating the system, just remember:

Your time will come.

You will be caught, and I hope the system comes down on you as hard as allowed by the civil and criminal laws of the land. For everybody else (and this applies, I hope, to everyone reading these words right now):

THIS IS YOUR TICKET
TO REGAINING YOUR SANITY.

THIS IS YOUR TICKET
TO REGAINING SOME DIGNITY.

THIS IS YOUR CHANCE TO REBUILD YOUR LIFE
BY GETTING THE DEBT COLLECTORS TO JUST . . .

BACK OFF!

Remember . . .

"Tough times don't last.
Tough people do."
Old Texas proverb

All right, folks . . . Let's get to work.

CONTENTS

1

IT STARTED
WITH GOOD INTENTIONS

"Courage is grace under pressure."
Ernest Hemingway

So how did it happen to you?

Did you get sick? Were you injured or involved in an automobile accident? Maybe you lost your job. Got your walking papers. Were laid off.

Whatever you call it, you're out of work and **out of cash**.

What about your former business partners? Did they rip you off? Run your business—and your life savings—into the ground?

Did you go through a messy divorce? Catch your spouse cheating on you? Maybe **you** got caught with your hand in the cookie jar.

How about all of that cheap money you borrowed to fit 4 years of college into 5 or 6 years? Having problems finding a job? Problems making ends meet? What about all of those "pre-approved" credit cards you took advantage of while you were still in college and didn't have any visible means of support? It's time to pay the piper!

Did your friends at VISA and MasterCard facilitate your doom? Maybe it was your own stupidity . . . your own irresponsibility. It felt like free money, didn't it?

That bright, shiny, new credit card with your name on it. And here was the best news of all: you could buy your groceries with it, buy movie tickets with it, go to Burger King and feed the kids with it . . . and if your limit allowed, you could get fresh, crisp, brand new money at any of 1,000,000 automated teller locations around the world with it.

Does any of this sound familiar to you?

It really doesn't matter how you painted yourself into the corner. You're in and you're in deep. How do you get out now? What should you do? Do you file for bankruptcy? It looks and sounds easy enough—those wonderful ads that run in the TV guide included in your Sunday newspaper that sell the ease of Chapter 13 or Chapter 7 and the attorney's willingness to take install-ment payments. They're selling you the hope of getting out of all of those debts, keep your home, keep your car . . . and rid yourself of your friends at the IRS.

Wake up, Dorothy! You're not in Kansas anymore.

It's just not that easy.

You **will** pay the price for taking the bankruptcy route for years to come, and contrary to what many "informed" attorneys tell you, a bankruptcy may buy you time with the IRS but it won't get rid of them in most cases!

I made some stupid mistakes back in the 1980s. Unfortunately, my mistakes were exacerbated by the Texas economy going in the tank, which made any chance for a rapid comeback even more difficult.

But *I* came back . . . and so can you.

It's time to wake up. Time to learn about the laws of the land. Time to learn from someone who's been there.

Here's reality:

Financial difficulties touch every socio-economic group in America at one time or another. It doesn't matter what your educational background is (believe me, I've seen many doctors, lawyers and professional types up to their rear in alligators). Your skin color or religion make no difference, and nobody cares about your political views or the type of car your drive. Simply stated, there's two types of consumers: Those with financial problems and those that are *going to have* financial problems. Sooner or later almost everyone will hit some rough roads in the world of money. How quick you recover, how fast you get back on your feet, and the level of brain damage you must endure have a direct correlation to your knowledge and insight into the world of the debt collector.

Their secrets, their motivations and their tactics are about to be revealed to the wrong group of people.

To you, the consumer.

Think of it this way: When you watch someone perform a card trick or a magician do a magic trick, it's pretty incredible. You can't figure out how they did it and you must admit that you're pretty amazed.

Until you learn the secret. Then it's not so amazing anymore, is it?

Believe me, it's the very same idea behind the world of the debt collector. They amaze you with the amount of information they know about you. They call you at

work, they call you at home. They'll call your neighbors, they'll call your family.

How did they know? How did they find you?

Stand by. Their secrets are about to be revealed and
you are about to turn the tables on the *#1 source of complaints to the Federal Trade Commission.*

You're about to learn how to level the playing field in
your battle for financial survival and sanity against those
tele-terrorists more commonly known as debt collectors.

2

THROWING GOOD MONEY AFTER BAD

"It's what you learn
after you know it all that counts."
John Wooden

Let's make one thing crystal clear.

This is not a how-to guide on getting out of your debts. This book is not intended to show consumers how to get out of paying bills they rightly owe. After all, if you don't pay your bills, everyone else ends up paying for it in the long run. Banks, mortgage companies and other creditors make up for their losses by raising prices for everyone else. Someone must pay.

However, there is a point in time when you must evaluate your personal dilemma without guilt and without emotion.

Anytime you make a decision based on emotion you increase the chance for that decision to be a major mistake. Debt collectors know this and prey on your emotions. They are extremely talented at pushing the right fear buttons in order to get you to sell your wedding ring. To get you to take that money that was allocated for food and wire it to them via Western Union. To get you to send them postdated checks from now until the turn of the century.

But for the average wage slave, other things come first—the . . .

House/rent payments

Electricity/utilities

Food

Insurance (homeowner's/health/auto)

The credit-card companies know that they're a lower priority in the big picture. They realize that they are not as important when a consumer is dealing with tough times financially. "We recognize that we're pretty far down the priority list," says Edward R. Sculy, vice president of First USA Bank, a Wilmington, Delaware subsidiary of Dallas-based First USA, Inc. "People are going to pay the rent and put food on the table before they pay credit-card companies. Our leverage is not that great."

With this knowledge in mind, the deals you work out with your ORIGINAL CREDITORS today could affect you for the next decade. It's absolutely crucial that you repay <u>ONLY</u> THE ORIGINAL CREDITOR. Never repay the debt collector. If the debt collector breaks you down and coerces you into paying them, you could be making a mistake that will haunt you for years to come. Let me explain.

Believe me, debt collectors are results-driven animals. They will say or do whatever it takes to get you to send them cash. They'll promise you that it will look better on your credit report. They'll promise to delete all negative information from your report if you repay them.

They'll rationalize until you get smart and question them, and then they'll revert to what they do best. Intimidate.

I urge you to repay your debts, but only to the original creditor. No matter what the debt collector tells you, you have the right under federal law to NOT deal with a third-party debt collector. You have the right to notify the debt collector that you wish to deal only with the original creditor.

If you break down and repay the first debt collector, this act of goodwill but uninformed weakness will:

a) Open you up to repeated harassment at the hands of the debt collector
b) Set you up for negative information for 7 years from the date you pay the debt off!
c) Set you up to potentially owe the debt to the original creditor, even if you've already paid the debt collector!

There's a handful of major "national" debt collection agencies. Chances are good that sooner or later your account(s) will end up going through one of these agencies, and with the powerful databases they use everyday, they'll compile a file on you so quick you won't know what hit you. And you can bet your debt collector pay history will show up in this file.

According to a recent interpretation from the Federal Trade Commission, information regarding your account may be reported for 7 years from the date of last activity. The date of last activity is either the date of last charge (on your original account) or date of last payment.

Hello? Are you listening?

I said <u>7</u> years from the date of last payment.

That means that if you defaulted on an account in January '88 it would "fall off" your credit report (if you did nothing about it) in January '95. However, if you tried to "do the right thing" and settle with the debt collector and in fact repaid the debt collector in full in January '94, that debt can now be reported on your credit report until January **2001!** You'd be penalized from 1988 through 2001 . . . 13 years for this mistake!

Is that fair?

Of course not.

Does it happen?

All the time.

How do you avoid it?

Read on. Knowledge is power!

Here's an absolutely true story that will shock you:

A debt collection agency in Texas collected a debt for one of their creditor/clients and then went bankrupt. The debt collector misappropriated the funds they collected and failed to repay these monies to the creditors.

The original creditor sues the debtor because they never received their money.

The debtor shows the creditor that they paid the debt collector, but the creditor wins in court and now, the debtor must pay the debt . . . **TWICE!**

Sound unfair?

Life is unfair. And justice is blind . . . and sometimes deaf and dumb. So do yourself a favor. Avoid the brain damage. Repay your debts on **your** terms. Repay your debts to the original creditor . . . never pay a debt collector!

3

DON'T EVEN THINK ABOUT BANKRUPTCY

*"A trifling debt makes a man your debtor,
a large one makes him your enemy."*
Seneca

It sure sounds good, doesn't it?

You know what I'm talking about. Those huge billboards urging consumers like you to:

"WIPE THE SLATE CLEAN!"

Those signs on the sides of buses and subways that say:

"HOW DO YOU SPELL RELIEF?
B-A-N-K-R-U-P-T-C-Y"

Those big display ads in the Sunday newspaper television guide that say:

"START FRESH! NO MORE IRS WORRIES!"

Perhaps you'll also remember the old saying:

"If it sounds too good to be true, it usually is!"

This is the one line you do need to believe.

Bankruptcy isn't what it's cracked up to be. Trust me. I've talked to thousands of consumers across the nation that regret filing for bankruptcy. Why? Because they misunderstood the long-term impact of taking bankruptcy. Things didn't work out as slick as the bankruptcy attorney promised. They weren't able to discharge all of their IRS debts. They didn't get to keep all of their personal property. They weren't able to get financing for a home a year later, as they were promised.

It just didn't work out like they thought it would.

If you are tired of the harassing phone calls at work from debt collectors, read on! You are about to become empowered and armed to avoid the #1 reason consumers do file for bankruptcy.

THE ORIGINS OF BANKRUPTCY

From the Bible to England by way of Italy, bankruptcy has been around for a long, long time. Believe it or not, bankruptcy is mentioned in the Bible. Chapter 15 in the Book of Deuteronomy calls for the release of all debts every seven years. Ancient Roman law also had a form of bankruptcy, but today's federal laws governing bankruptcy go back five centuries. Under King Henry VIII laws were passed in England in 1542 that serve as the basis of today's U.S. Bankruptcy Code.

The word "bankruptcy" originated from the Italian term meaning "broken bench." According to early Italian customs, when a tradesman or merchant couldn't pay their debts, their workbench or display table was broken and displayed as a symbol of his failure.

THE TYPES OF BANKRUPTCY

As far as consumers are concerned, there are two types of bankruptcy. What a consumer may keep varies state to state. Even though the bankruptcy laws are federally administered, many states have kept certain exemptions that give the debtors additional rights and the ability to protect additional assets.

Texas and Florida are famous for their reputations as "debtors' havens" because of state exemptions that allow, for example, debtors to protect ALL of the equity in their homesteads (with the exception of property taxes and the IRS). Even if a debtor owns a $10 million home free and clear of all liens and owes $5 million to creditors (except for our friends at the IRS, child support and student loans) those creditors are left out in the cold in bankruptcy court. Many cash value life insurance policies, Individual Retirement Accounts, etc. are also exempt from creditors. Again, state laws regarding "exempt" versus "non-exempt" assets need to be considered when a debtor is considering filing for bankruptcy.

CHAPTER 7 bankruptcies are also known as "straight bankruptcies" or "liquidations." That means that all exempt assets and property is sold or liquidated and distributed to the creditors. If a consumer is going to make the decision to take a bankruptcy, it usually makes most sense to go ahead and liquidate EVERYBODY (but maybe not the IRS). That means that it's behind you and you do not have to make any future payments out of future income. If you're going to take the hit, you might as well make it count and finish it off.

CHAPTER 13 bankruptcies are also referred to as "Wage Earners." It allows the debtor to "adjust" their debts and work out a repayment schedule. The debtor is protected from lawsuits, garnishments and other creditor actions while under a Chapter 13 bankruptcy workout and has up to five years to repay their creditors. The only qualification for a debtor is that they must have a regular income, making commission sales people unable to qualify for this plan . . . and that might be a blessing in disguise.

The only real benefits to taking a Chapter 13 bankruptcy are these:

1) If you've already taken a Chapter 7 bankruptcy in the last six years, you're not eligible to file for another Chapter 7, but you could file a Chapter 13 bankruptcy petition;

2) If you have "non-dischargeable" debts such as some types of student loans or judgments resulting from criminal negligence or fraud;

3) The debtor is allowed to cure a default on a long-term debt, such as a mortgage contract;

4) A co-signor on a note that has been defaulted upon is protected;

5) Certain "non-exempt" property that would other-wise be liquidated by the courts in a Chapter 7 are protected;

6) Some may tell you that a Chapter 13 bankruptcy only stays on a credit report for seven (instead of ten) years and try to sell this as an advantage. It's better than ten years, but a bankruptcy on your credit report is still a negative and will follow you for the rest of your life.

Don't take this summary as the final word. Get qualified advice from a qualified individual who doesn't have something to gain from your final decision. An accountant. A successful family friend. Just heed my warnings and understand the long-term implications of your final decision.

TAKE THE CHAPTER 7!

If you're going to commit "financial suicide" by taking the bankruptcy route, then finish the job!

Chapter 13 bankruptcies are more expensive than Chapter 7 because they have to be administered by an attorney approved by the court for the duration of the bankruptcy protection until the case is discharged or dismissed. They need to be paid for their time, so the court protects their fee and includes this in your monthly budget.

A bankruptcy is a bankruptcy is a bankruptcy.

Once you file, regardless of the type, you've "filed for bankruptcy." Future creditors aren't going to give you "brownie points" for paying off your debt over a five-year period. They're going to focus on the fact that you filed for bankruptcy. Period.

If you file for a Chapter 13 bankruptcy and it is either dismissed by the court for some reason or you change your mind and withdraw the petition, it's too late. You have "filed for bankruptcy." It will show up at the courthouse. It will show up on your credit report for at least 10 years from the date the case is dismissed.

This reality should be easy enough to understand:

Don't get pulled down by your guilt about filing for bankruptcy and vow to "repay all of your creditors" and take the Chapter 13 route. In most cases, if your creditors are going to work with you, you'll never have to go to the courthouse. They'll work with you if you are honest and realistic, and won't force you to take a bankruptcy.

Don't get conned into taking the Chapter 13 route by your bankruptcy attorney. Remember, your attorney's the one that will be making the court-protected fee on your Chapter 13 petition for the next 5 years.

Other types of consumer bankruptcy include a **CHAPTER 12**, which is similar to a Chapter 13 except that it specifically relates to Family Farm Reorganizations. Financial circumstances surrounding working family ranches, farms, etc. need to be handled by a qualified bankruptcy expert, preferably someone that is board certified. Furthermore, the better debtors understand the system, the better off they will be. I urge anyone considering any type of bankruptcy to consider reading some of the books I list in the "Suggested Reading" section in the back of this book.

Another term you'll never find in the U.S. Bankruptcy Code but one you may hear is a **CHAPTER 20**. Some attorneys file a Chapter 13 petition to buy time, especially with secured creditors such as mortgage lien holders, let the dust settle, then convert the filing to a Chapter 7 liquidation. (Get it? A Chapter 13 plus a Chapter 7 adds up to . . . you guessed it . . . a Chapter 20.)

COMMON DEBTOR MISCONCEPTIONS

MISCONCEPTION NUMBER ONE: *"The only way I can get my creditors to stop calling me is to file for bankruptcy!"*

REALITY: In most cases, debtors are having to endure debt collector harassment. This will quickly evaporate once you've read **BACK OFF!** a couple of times and begun sending out Cease & Desist letters to the Third Party Debt Collectors that are making your life miserable.

If you're having to fade the heat of the original creditors, what's stopping you from changing your phone number? What's stopping you from getting a post office box? An assortment of "bulletproofing" ideas are waiting for you to put into action in the "Covering Your Assets" chapter of this book.

MISCONCEPTION NUMBER TWO: *"My attorney told me since my credit is already torn up, I might as well get the bankruptcy out of the way and start over fresh!"*

REALITY: Wrong. You didn't screw up your credit overnight . . . you're not going to clean it up overnight, either. Get your hands on a copy of my book **LIFE AFTER DEBT**, which focuses on the holes in the credit reporting system, and get your credit information back under control.

And don't forget, if you file for bankruptcy, your attorney gets his court-protected fee. He makes his money and you're just another bankruptcy filing to add to his files. Remember, attorneys make money when they litigate.

MISCONCEPTION NUMBER THREE: *"I've got some credit cards paid off . . . some have small balances that I've been paying on. I'll get rid of the big balances and big creditors by taking bankruptcy."*

REALITY: What have you been smoking?

First off, it is very common for credit card companies like American Express to do "spot checks" on their cardholders. These spot checks can come at any time for any reason, although they do use a scoring system that is fairly successful in predicting which consumers will have financial problems. In the meantime, if a company like American Express should pull a copy of your credit report and find that you have filed for bankruptcy, they'll revoke your privileges in a heartbeat. It doesn't matter that you've charged and paid $100,000 since your bankruptcy. If they find out that something has developed in your financial situation that doesn't fit in with their cardholder profile guidelines, your card is history. Believe me, these revocations can occur at the most embarrassing moments.

Secondly, you must list all of your outstanding creditors. That means even if you owe only $20 to VISA, you must list them on your petition. Once that creditor has been notified that they're being contacted by a bankruptcy court about your bankruptcy action, you can just about count down the seconds to the time they turn your card off and pick it up.

Finally, don't think you're going to selectively keep certain obligations in bankruptcy court. If the judge or trustee detects you're playing games, you can be charged with "Substantial Abuse" and your entire bankruptcy petition thrown out. You only thought you had problems before.

MISCONCEPTION NUMBER FOUR: *"I was told that bankruptcy only lasts seven years and that I'll be able to get credit again after only a year or two, especially since I won't owe anything!"*

REALITY: Normal "bad credit" can stay on a credit report for seven years. Bankruptcies can stay on your credit report for ten years after they've been discharged. Don't think that just because your bankruptcy is "behind" you and you owe no money to creditors that it will be easy to re-enter the credit community. Every creditor has their own credit-granting guidelines, but suffice it to say that you will be turned down more often than you'll be approved. And if you are approved, in most cases you will pay a premium over what a consumer who had never filed for bankruptcy would pay.

SOME CLOSING THOUGHTS
ABOUT BANKRUPTCY

Sometimes, taking a bankruptcy is the only way out . . . like when that woman ran me over with her car.

I didn't tell you about that? Here's the story, quick and simple: This woman hits me, I endure 20 visits to the hospital and 12 surgeries and some permanent damage and, you guessed it, it was her fault. Instead of watching what she was doing, she took 3 years out of my life because of her ineptitude behind the wheel. I sued her and got a $723,000 judgment . . . and she promptly filed a bankruptcy petition before the ink was even dry on my judgment. Why did she do it?

Because she knew that as mad as I was, I would follow her to her grave. I would offset every bank account and seize every non-exempt asset she or husband would *ever* have, and I'd be their worst nightmare. I'd follow her to her grave for every penny she owed me. She was smart in taking the bankruptcy.

But this case is the exception, not the rule. I've had many friends in the real estate business take bankruptcy because their debts were so large (in excess of $5 million) that they knew they could preserve enough of their assets (legally) through state exemptions and the use of children's and family trusts, etc. They knew that they could start over with fewer problems and more assets than 98% of all debtors that file for bankruptcy.

Is this wrong? It's not my job to pass moral or ethical judgments. It's my job to inform consumers of their rights. Every individual must make their own choices.

Is your choice to file for bankruptcy driven by an intimidating stream of phone calls and threatening letters? You mean you still haven't figured out by now that this book will save you from this type of harassment?

Never file bankruptcy just to end the calls and threats from the debt collection industry. This book is your ticket to sanity and control. Keep reading . . .

4

DEBT COLLECTORS: TODAY'S TELE-TERRORISTS

"Greed is good."
Gordon Gekko, from the movie Wall Street

These guys are great.

They know how to scare you into doing what's best for them, not you. They know how to use the phone as a weapon. Some will insinuate, others will be much more bold. Threats of the sheriff showing up at your door. Threats of arrest at your place of employment. Threats of getting the courts to turn over custody of your children, since obviously you can't handle responsibility.

I'm not kidding. These people recover money for their clients using *whatever* trick in the book that works for them. I'm not making this up. I've talked to thousands of consumers who have shared their horror stories with me.

But here's the good news:

They can't do anything to you. They can't do anything more than, at the very worst, get a judgment against you. If they have security (like an automobile or home loan) they can always repossess the item you financed. In most states the creditor will be able to garnish your wages. But let's face it, you can't get blood out of a turnip. If you can't pay them, you can't pay them. It's costly to go to court. It's costly to get an attorney to jump through all of the hoops to garnish your paycheck. If you're self-employed, it's going to be tough for them to get you to garnish yourself. If you're in commission sales, it's just as difficult.

You should avoid letting it get to this stage at all costs. Take the debt collector out of the picture early and go back and deal with the original creditor.

GREED DRIVES THE COLLECTOR

The debt collection industry thrives on greed. With revenues approaching $80 billion, it's no wonder that the debt collectors around the nation are so aggressive.

Since most creditors assign their overdue accounts to debt collectors on a contingency basis, all it costs the debt collector is the time to call up debtors and scare the money out of them. (A contingency basis means that the collector promises to collect on a "best efforts" basis. The creditor doesn't owe anything to the collector unless the collector collects. The collector doesn't earn any commission unless they are successful in collecting the debt. Therein lies the incentive . . . the more the debt collector collects, the more money they make.)

Here's a classic example: Suppose you owe Rody's Department Store $1,000. The account receivables department at Rody's tries to collect the account for 90, maybe 120 days before they deem the account uncollectible.

(PLEASE NOTE: If the internal accounting/collections department at Rody's is trying to collect your overdue account, NONE of the Cease & Desist letters in this book will work. Since Rody's is the original creditor, all bets are off. The strategies outlined in *BACK OFF!* work only when dealing with outside, THIRD PARTY DEBT COLLECTORS. There have been some discussions about trying to get the same protection afforded by the Fair Debt Collection Practices Act to cover the activities of original creditors against consumers . . . but it hasn't happened yet.)

The fuse length of the in-house collections department of the original creditor is fairly predictable. They'll rarely try to collect past due accounts longer than 120 days, but I have heard some cases of original creditors trying to collect past due accounts for up to 240 to 270 days. Sooner or later, if they can't collect the account, the original creditor will consider the account "uncollectible."

Once they consider the account uncollectible they "charge off" the account. This means they can now deduct the monies you owe them as a "Bad Debt Expense" which offsets their taxable income. At the same time they'll report this account as "UNCOL-LECTIBLE," "CHARGE OFF" or "COLLECTION ACCOUNT" to at least one of the national credit reporting bureaus (our friends at TRW, CSC/Equifax or TransUnion) and you're stuck with this negative information on your credit report for at least 7 years (and maybe more if you handle this situation incorrectly).

When Rody's charged off your account they pooled it with other overdue accounts and assigned it to a debt collection agency, maybe a local agency . . . probably a national company. Your account ended up in the hands of Vito's Collection Agency with the understanding that Vito's would collect as much of the debt as quickly as possible. The account was assigned on a BEST EFFORTS BASIS . . . a very important point to remember.

INCENTIVE IS THE NAME OF THE GAME

The account was **assigned**, not sold.

It is very rare that the debt collection agency actually owns the account, meaning they bought it from the original creditor. More than likely, it was assigned to Vito's, which means they're considered THIRD PARTY DEBT COLLECTORS and their collection methods are restricted by the Fair Debt Collection Practices Act, which I'll discuss in greater detail in Chapter 8.

For this example we'll assume that your account is assigned to one of Vito's top debt collectors, a person by the name of Richard Head. Mr. Head has plenty of incentive to collect the account for Rody's Department Store . . . about 250 reasons. If you were to repay the $1,000 to Mr. Head at Vito's Collection Agency, this is how the money would be split:

$500 given to Rody's Department Store (original creditor)

$250 kept by Vito's Collection Agency

$250 given to Richard Head, Debt Collection Agent

Not only is your new best friend Richard Head making a nice commission for harassing you on the phone several times a week—maybe even daily—but now he's going to put negative lines of information on your credit report that will stay for a minimum of 7 years! I think it would be a better idea to take Mr. Head and his associates at Vito's Collection Agency out of the collection loop forever. And if the original creditor assigns your overdue account to another debt collection agency, take them out, too! Read on. *BACK OFF!* shows you how to eliminate the debt collectors from the collection equation.

By the way, the average debt collector can maintain dozens of accounts like yours on an ongoing basis. In other words, if they're hammering people like you successfully across the nation and collecting $10,000 a week for clients of their agency, that means the agency is keeping $5,000 a week generated by that ONE individual collector. That one collector, Richard Head in this example, is making $2,500 a week. That's $10,000 a month. Or $120,000 a year. The incentive to be aggressive is obvious. That's why you've got to eliminate the debt collector from your life. Forever.

OH MY GOD! AN ATTORNEY IS HARASSING ME!

Oh no! You've received a collection letter from a law firm. Your worst nightmare has come true . . . the attorneys are after you! Now they'll sue you for sure, they'll call your boss, they'll call your neighbors, they'll have you thrown in jail . . .

Wrong.

Here's the **great** news!

Any attorney that collects two or more debts a year is (you guessed it) a debt collector!

That means their activities are also regulated by the Fair Debt Collection Practices Act, and they can also be eliminated from the collection equation by using the Cease & Desist Letter in Appendix C of this book.

Don't get carried away here: the attorneys can always file suit against you on behalf of their client, the original creditor. But remember, you can't get blood out of a turnip and if you had the money in the first place, you would have paid them. Right? So the attorneys can always sue you, but they're not stupid. It's unlikely they'll throw good money after bad. If they take a look at your credit bureau report and see that your entire report is torn up and you owe everybody and their brother, they know it's going to be tough to collect anything from you even if they do get a judgment.

I have seen debtors owing $10-15,000 threatened but never sued. So relax. Take the attorney from the (debt collection) law firm of Bandini, Lambert & Locke out of the game with the same Cease & Desist Letter located in Appendix C in the back of this book.

NOT EVERY COLLECTOR IS NASTY

Fortunately, one of the nation's largest credit card issuers is waking up and coming to the realization that the old adage may be true:

> *"You catch more flies with honey*
> *than you do with vinegar."*

Here's a case in point.

In the Monday, June 27, 1994 edition of *The Wall Street Journal* an article on page B1 focuses on the kinder, gentler collection techniques now being utilized by Chase Manhattan Bank. When a customer has "gone underground" or "skipped," they no longer send out a threatening letter. They send out a videotape. In an amazing change of strategy, the tape drips with kindness and understanding. "Even though you're in collection, you're still our customer," says the commentator. "You're still #1 with us."

Fantastic! They're finally wising up!

Now if they'll only be reasonable when you try to work out new terms with them, they'll have this puzzle solved. Creditors like Chase Manhattan should be applauded for trying civilized techniques to collect overdue accounts. But once a debtor does call in and is attempting to re-negotiate repayment terms, creditors like Chase had better realize that thanks in part to books that I have written like *BACK OFF!* or *LIFE AFTER DEBT*, today's consumer is smarter than ever.

This isn't meant to be a self-serving pat on the back for me. I'm simply pointing out that today's consumers are better informed about the system and the laws that govern debt collections and credit reporting.

If a consumer is willing to repay a debt but not willing to be penalized for the next 7 years with negative information on their credit bureau report, then the original creditors of the land like Chase Manhattan Bank had better realize that they're going to have to do more than schmooze debtors in collection with videotapes and sweetness.

Today's informed consumer knows that the creditor can remove negative information from a credit bureau report. When the representative on the 800 number tells the consumer that they can't remove this information once the debt has been repaid because it's against the law, *they're lying*.

The original creditor put the information there. They can remove it. If they want their money, they'd better agree to delete any negative information placed on your credit report by their company or any debt collection agency they hired to try to collect the account.

If they don't agree to remove this information, they don't get paid. It's just that simple. **Remember the Golden Rule:**

"He who has the gold, rules."

In this case, the consumer has the gold. The consumer has what the debt collector want. Money. As long as you've got the cash, you've got the leverage to negotiate how this account shows up on your credit report for at least the next 7 years. Once you've repaid the money you owe, you have no hammer . . . you have no leverage. The creditors will negotiate, but only the informed consumer will have the chance. "We don't like to advertise it, but we will reduce fees and interest," says Joseph J. Giuseffi, Chase Manhattan's nationwide collections chief. "We find that if you forgive fees and some interest, people are more likely to complete the repayment programs."

According to Kenneth R. Crone, VISA USA's vice president for consumer risk: "The people who success-fully complete a repayment program rarely go into bankruptcy." You've got the leverage. Don't ever forget it. And don't be swayed by sweet videotapes.

If you don't believe me, read the article in *The Wall Street Journal*. According to John A. Ward III, the head of Chase's credit-card business, the stakes are high: "Of Chase's $9.7 billion in credit-card loans, 5.6% of $543 million is more than 60 days past due."

A LOOK BEHIND THE SCENES

A couple of years ago I attended a seminar sponsored by a nationally recognized debt collection agency. The seminar was directed towards the medical community, giving office managers ideas on collecting medical bills.

Their very informative "Collecting in the '90s" semi-nar highlighted many basic concepts in the world of debt collection, including the TIME-VALUE concept of receivables. The general feeling when collecting med-ical bills or any other unsecured receivable is simple enough. The older the bill is, the longer it takes to col-lect the debt that directly translates into the net amount of money the creditor expects to receive.

Let me make one thing clear: If you owe the money, **you need to pay it**. The more you pay on the bill the better it is for everyone involved in the equation. The creditor deserves to be paid for their monies loaned or goods and services you've received. After all, if you don't pay your bill, the creditor will end up passing along their losses in the form of higher prices to everyone else. Whether it's doctors' fees, higher prices at your favorite department store, or higher bank charges and interest rates from the credit card companies, your local savings and loan, credit union, or bank . . . we all will end up paying the price.

But if you're out of cash and you can't pay, there's really nothing left to discuss. However, if you can pay something instead of nothing (which frequently occurs in bankruptcy), then this softens the overall impact to society. Something **is** better than nothing.

Here's what the folks in the medical receivable industry expect (according to their past experience) to collect on their past due account:

MONTHS PAST DUE	PERCENT LOSS	DOLLAR VALUE
3 months	10%	90¢
4 months	14%	86¢
5 months	19%	81¢
6 months	33%	67¢
12 months	55%	45¢
24 months	77%	23¢
36 months	85%	15¢
48 months	88%	12¢
60 months	*forget it!*	*practically worthless*

I only show you this schedule to illustrate an important point. The health care providers are expecting to receive less than 100 cents of every dollar owed. If they assign your account to a debt collection agency, they are expecting even less, since the debt collector will receive a commission equal to 30-50% of every overdue dollar they collect. This means that (now armed with this knowledge) you need to negotiate with the original creditor. Don't even let it get to the debt collector stage . . . work out restructured repayment terms with the original creditor (in this example, the health care provider) whenever possible and stick to those new terms.

A STRATEGY WORTH REPEATING

Part of your leverage when negotiating with the creditors is the fact that they know that you can always end all of the madness and file for bankruptcy. You're not really going to file (unless extreme circumstances dictate) but this is about your only hammer when trying to re-structure your financial situation. This is your "big threat." The debt collector and even original creditor may threaten you with a lawsuit, but you can counter with the threat of bankruptcy. They are always entitled to sue you for not paying your debt, but you can always take them into bankruptcy court—in which case they'll end up with, at best, pennies on the dollar . . . and in most cases they'll receive nothing.

So that's your leverage. Remember to use it.

SKIPTRACING: BIG BROTHER WANTS YOU TO *THINK* HE'S WATCHING YOU

As you know by now, the debt collector is very good at using all the information at their disposal to intimidate you. These intimidation techniques generate collections, and in turn big commissions, to the debt collector.

Skiptracing is the term used to track down debtors who have dropped out of sight or have unlisted their phone number and become difficult to communicate with. The debt collection industry classifies these "skips," placing them into one of four categories:

- Unintentional skips
- Skips resulting from marital difficulties
- Intentional skips
- Skips with criminal intent

In my opinion (and this is verified by statistics) the "skips with criminal intent" are a very small percentage. Most people go "underground" for one of the other three reasons, and I'd like to add a fifth category. How about skips *afraid* of the size of the medical bills they're buried under? Let's not forget, medical bills have become the #1 reason Americans have been filing for bankruptcy in recent years.

Here are some facts that collection agencies don't want you to know, courtesy of that seminar I attended a few years ago:

1) One out of every five people move to a new address every year.

2) Up to 50% of all accounts collected by collection agencies require some form of skiptracing.

3) Skiptracing helps reduce/decrease bad debt losses.

4) Skiptracing helps the collection agency:

a) Locate the debtor in hopes of collecting.

b) Determine if the debtor is able to pay up.

c) Determine if other creditors are pursuing the same debtor.

d) Determine what the debtor's paying habits are.

e) Determine the stability of the debtor's employment.

5) Here's the magic question: Should the creditor or debt collector pursue the skip? These are a few guidelines they follow in making that decision:

a) Use good judgment (sometimes a rare commodity in this profession) and follow all state and federal laws.

b) Virtually every debtor can be located with sufficient time and expenditure of money.

c) Creditors must limit the amount of time and money spent in order to keep skiptracing costs in line with the size of the debt.

d) Keep potential recovery in mind.

e) Skiptrace in order to locate someone who will pay the account, not just to gather information.

Re-read items 5 c-e! These are extremely important points of the collection equation to remember. Creditors and debt collectors are NOT going to throw good money after bad. These people are not going to waste their time chasing and harassing someone if they think their chance of recovery is slim to none. Their time is money, too!

SO YOU WANT TO KNOW HOW THEY FOUND YOU?

Computers have sure made the debt collector's job easier, and made them more effective. But even with the assistance of computers and massive consumer data bases, the typical debt collector has a predictable pattern they follow to track down "skips."

Let's take the mystery out of their magic. Let's eliminate the fear of the unknown by showing you the very same checklist the debt collectors follow when they're attempting to locate consumers that may have gone "underground." Here are the techniques the debt collection community uses to find anyone and everyone.

LOCATION INFORMATION
   a) The debtor's last place of residence.
   b) The last telephone number at that place of residence.
   c) The debtor's last place of employment.

INFORMATION TO BE DEVELOPED/
CONFIRMED ON SKIPS
   a) The debtor's name, including the correct and complete spelling of the debtor's full name, middle initial, junior or senior, etc.

b) The debtor's correct address, including correct street name, number and zip code (9-digit preferred).

c) The debtor's previous address.

d) The debtor's place of employment, including their occupation (remember, debtors usually stay within their trade or occupation).

e) Debtors who are members of trade unions, school-teachers, nurses, etc. are relatively easy to find if you can figure out where they may have moved to.

f) Obtain information about debtor's position, length of employment, earnings, usual paydays, etc.

g) If you are dealing with a former employer, quiz them in order to obtain any references or find out if anyone else has made any inquiries since the debtor has left. Posing as a friend from "back home," high school or college is an effective ruse, as is posing as a relative.

h) Find out if the debtor rents, leases or owns property.

i) If the debtor does own any real estate, check public records (courthouse or tax rolls) for the name of the mortgagor.

j) Once you find out the mortgagor, you may be able to find out by contacting them directly who carries the insurance on the property—another potential wealth of information and leads.

k) If the debtor rents, find out the landlord or property, management company's name, address and telephone number—on-site property managers will talk in many cases.

l) Check to see if debtor owns an automobile or motor-cycle through department of motor vehicle records.

m) Obtain name, address and telephone number of company that financed or currently has a lien on the automobile.

n) Get out the criss-cross directory. Former neighbors are usually a pretty good source of information. See next category for line of questioning.

o) Current neighbors: A terrific source of information! When does the debtor go to work? What time do they come home? What type of car do they drive? Can you get a license number? Do you know what they do for a living? Do they have any kids? Have you ever talked with them? What did they have to say?

SKIPTRACING BY MAIL

a) Remember, a debt collection agency may not send correspondence through the mail that indicates the sender is a debt collector.

b) The Post Office will search their records and give you the new address, if one exists, for $1.00.

c) The Post Office is also a pretty good source of information to get additional data on the debtor (if they rented) by tracing the 9-digit zip code. These 9-digit zips can supply more specific data that can be used for further tracing.

d) Try mailing an empty envelope (with your return mailing address) to the last known address with the notation in the bottom right-hand corner "POSTMASTER: FORWARDING AND ADDRESS CORRECTION REQUESTED." If there is a forwarding address the post office will send this information to you for (currently) a 25¢ fee.

e) "RETURN TO SENDER" is your first sign of trouble and indicates your debtor is probably a skip.

f) Carefully examine all returned mail that is undeliverable for clues.

g) "NOT HERE" is a typical Post Office wording that indicates the debtor is no longer there.

h) "NOT THERE" is not normally used by the Post Office and indicates it was probably written by someone still at that address.

i) "MOVED-NO FORWARDING ADDRESS" indicates the debtor is probably a true skip.

j) "FORWARDING ORDER EXPIRED" indicates the time limit for forwarding has run out (you may get lucky and check with the post office and get a copy of the forwarding order).

k) "CERTIFIED MAIL/RETURN RECEIPT REQUESTED" is useful when you need confirmation of a piece of mail being delivered and also to verify who signed for it.

l) "RESTRICTED DELIVERY" assures that the target debtor receives the mail. This is a premium service and costs extra.

m) "FORWARD" will show the target debtor's new address if on file and will show the return item from the post office.

n) "RETURN TO SENDER IF NOT DELIVERED ON FIRST ATTEMPT" is used if you are trying to keep from tipping your hand that you are searching for the target debtor. Without this instruction, your target will be able to claim the letter at the post office and will know that you're looking for them. In addition, you still would not have a certified address.

SKIPTRACING BY TELEPHONE

a) Making telephone contact is the most effective, fastest and cheapest method.

b) Use good timing when contacting your informants in order to gain their maximum cooperation. Don't forget the time, place and type of person you are attempting to contact.

c) Avoid calling early in the morning, when your informant is trying to get kids to school and themselves to work, or at dinnertime.

d) Always leave a phone number (preferably toll-free) for informants to call you back.

e) Identify your informant. Always know who you are talking to and verify their name and address.

f) Identify yourself, stating only your name. Don't identify your employer, unless they specifically ask you to do so. If informant asks you to identify your employer, simply state the name of the original creditor (not your Collection Agency name).

g) Tell your informant you need their help. Be courteous and friendly. Try to build a rapport with your informant immediately . . . this will encourage them to respond.

h) Under the Fair Debt Collection Practices Act (Public Law 95-109) you can only contact your target debtor at their place of residence, their place of employment or the telephone number you have on record.

i) Use psychology on your informant. Silently wait for them to make the next move. Wait for them to respond. Be patient.

j) Listen closely for information and leads. Analyze everything the informant says to you since they may give you leads to other sources of information.

k) Analyze the informant's attitude. Be alert for inavertent clues and listen closely for inconsistencies.

l) Question your informant. Your questions may help turn up more information than the informant realizes they know. Limit your questions to acquisition of location information. Be sure to phrase all of your questions in a positive manner. Sound confident that you have the right information, even though you may be attempting to bluff information out of your informant.

m)Be prepared for any questions your prospective informant may have for you. You should try to structure all of your answers with a combination answer and counter-question of your own. This counter-question will usually prevent the informant from asking you any additional questions. If the informant should ask, tell them that you need to contact the debtor about a business matter.

n) Close your call. As soon as you have all of the information you want or all you think you can get from this particular informant, end the call.

o) Don't allow time for the informant to ask you too many questions. Take your information and end the call.

ADDITIONAL SOURCES OF INFORMATION

a) Old and new telephone directories.

b) Criss-cross directories. One section lists households and businesses by street name and number; another section lists all telephone numbers by exchange and lists to whom that number is assigned.

c) City directories. Information obtained by direct canvassing of the city by mail, phone and sometimes even personal contacts. Most residents of the city are included, even those with unlisted phone numbers. City directories are usually divided into four sections:

- Business and professional firms
- Names of residents and businesses listed alphabetically
- Listing of households and businesses by street name
- Telephone numbers (in numerical order) followed by the names and addresses of the person(s) or business(es) to whom the telephones are listed

WHO DO YOU CONTACT?

a) Go back through all/old files on debtor.

b) Contact former or current neighbors.

c) Contact former or current friends.

d) Contact relatives.

e) Former employers.

f) Apartment managers or landlords.

g) Local stores, service stations, barber/beauty shops, restaurants or bars the debtor may have frequented.

h) Social services agencies.

i) Schools, alumni associations, PTAs, etc.

PUBLIC RECORDS/PUBLIC DOMAIN

a) Review any divorce actions at the courthouse. These usually turn up some great information on your target. Besides . . . ex-spouses usually enjoy making the lives of their former wives/husbands miserable.

b) Real estate contracts.

c) Bankruptcies (another treasure trove of insight and information).

d) Liens.

e) Foreclosures.

f) Homestead declarations.

g) Probate of estates.

h) Building permits.

i) Chattel mortgages.

j) Deeds of all kinds.

k) Tax liens . . . state and federal.

ADDITIONAL RESEARCH AREAS

a) Local newspapers.

b) City, county and state maps.

c) Social Security Numbers. Analyze and identify area of country number was issued and the approximate date of issue.

d) Chamber of Commerce membership directories. Locate either target debtor or former/current employer(s).

e) Military base directories.

f) High school/college student/faculty directories.

g) Labor unions.

h) Finance companies.

i) Utility companies.

j) Cable television companies.

k) Credit bureau reports.

l) Moving companies.

m)Check with lienholder on current automobile.

n) Real estate tax rolls.

o) Birth and death records.

p) Motor vehicle records.

q) Criminal or civil records.

r) Libraries! Terrific sources of information, now available through computer on-line searches, CD-ROM archives, etc.

ARMED FORCES RECORDS

a) Write to each branch of the service and ask for the address of your missing debtor. If the target debtor was never in the service, they'll let you know. If they were and they have a current address, they'll pass that along for a nominal fee. Many times they may have their last known address which is many times a new lead, or the address of a relative or friend.

b) Enclose a payment (currently) of $2.40 for each address requested.

c) Be sure to include the Social Security Number of the debtor to speed their information search.

d) Include the city or town from which the debtor entered the service, if known.

e) If you don't know which branch of the service the debtor joined, try the U.S. Army first, since it is the largest branch of the military.

f) In order, send your requests to the Army, Navy, Air Force, Coast Guard, Marines and Merchant Marine.

THE MISTAKE OF OPENING A DIALOGUE WITH THE DEBT COLLECTOR: WHAT TO EXPECT

So you won't be shocked or surprised by the dialogue those wonderful debt collectors will attempt to engage you in, here are some scenarios you will most likely encounter and the impact of making the wrong choices:

SCENARIO #1: "You can't pay the original creditor anymore!" the debt collector insists. "You had your chance to pay them and you didn't! Now they've turned this account over to our company. They won't accept your payments. You must pay our offices!"

REALITY: Many times the original creditor will turn over large groups of past-due accounts to the debt collection agency with the agreement that all payments received by the original creditor's office will be turned over to the debt collector. The debt collector's job is to collect those accounts and they'll receive their money regardless of whom you pay.

THE "DOVER-SMART" CONSUMER'S SOLUTION: Eliminate the debt collection agency by invoking federal law by utilizing the Cease & Desist Letter (Appendix C) located in the back of this book. Never pay the debt collector!

MOST PROBABLE NEGATIVE IMPACT OF PAYING THE DEBT COLLECTOR: The debt collector may remove only the negative information their debt collection agency placed on your credit report. The debt collector cannot remove any information placed there by the original creditor. If they promise you they can, they're lying.

SCENARIO #2: "If you send our offices six post-dated checks," says the debt collector, "we'll not only cease all collection activity, we'll consider giving you a 20-30% discount on the amount of money you owe us!"

REALITY: One of their favorite tools of the trade is the post-dated check. Some debt collection agencies will hold the checks until the date you've dated on them. Some debt collectors don't care and will try to cash the checks sooner, especially if they're having a slow collections month. It also gives them that unspoken leverage that if you bounce a check, not only will your bank penalize you for at least $20, the debt collector will get the district attorney's office involved and have you put in jail.

THE "DOVER-SMART" CONSUMER'S SOLUTION: Eliminate the debt collection agency by invoking federal law by utilizing the Cease & Desist Letter (Appendix C). Never pay the debt collector!

MOST PROBABLE NEGATIVE IMPACT OF PAY-ING THE DEBT COLLECTOR: If you were foolish enough to send the debt collector these checks and something happens that causes one of those checks to bounce (i.e., a late paycheck, a child gets sick, the car breaks down), you not only have the bank taking your hard-earned money for Non-Sufficient Funds fees, but you're now inviting the debt collector to turn up the heat of harassment that they routinely use in the collection of overdue accounts, in addition to your name being added to the BAD CHECK BLACKLIST. Remember, never pay the debt collector!

SCENARIO #3: "Tell you what," says the debt collector. "You go down and send me $50 now via Western Union and I'll get my boss to hold this account long enough for you to get things worked out!"

REALITY: You'll be flushing that $50 down the toilet. The minute they receive that cash they'll turn the heat up. They'll come up with some other reason to get you to send them another $25, another $50. By the way, Western Union has a deal they've worked out with debt collectors across the nation to get money into their hands quickly. Western Union at one point even developed incentives and prizes for debt collectors that utilized their services to win! They've stacked the deck against you! You can't win if you deal with the debt collector.

THE "DOVER-SMART" CONSUMER'S SOLUTION: Tell the debt collector that your friend/brother/ sister is going to write a check for you. They'll send them $100 . . . $200 . . .but you need to get the debt collector's name, their company name, their address, etc. You're borrowing the money and you've got to do what the person lending you the money tells you. "So if you want the money, Mr. Debt Collector, you'd better give me this information so we can express mail this check to you!" Then send the debt collector the Cease & Desist Letter (Appendix C) via certified mail. See you later! Never pay the debt collector!

__MOST PROBABLE NEGATIVE IMPACT OF PAY-
ING THE DEBT COLLECTOR__: You've wasted whatever money you've scraped together and opened yourself up for continued harassment. You're screwed.

__SCENARIO #4__: You get an "important" phone call at
work. "You know you're not supposed to get phone
calls while you're working!" your boss tells you as you
pick up the phone.

"Hello?"

"Listen, pal. If you don't get that money you owe
Rody's Department Store to me by 5:00 this afternoon
I'm calling your boss back tomorrow and tell him that
he's got a thief working for him! I'm not kidding. You
get that money out to me via Western Union or else he
gets my next call!"

__REALITY__: The debt collector has already (surprise)
broken federal law by threatening you with something
they can't do! It is illegal to discuss your account with
any unrelated third party (like your boss, your neighbor,
your mother or father, etc.).

__THE "DOVER-SMART" CONSUMER'S SOLUTION__:
Act terrified and tell the debt collector that your
friend/brother/sister is going to write a check for you.
They'll send them $100 . . . $200 . . . but you need to get
the debt collector's name, their company name, their
address, etc. Tell them that you're borrowing the money
and you've got to do what the person lending you the
money tells you. "So if you want the money, Mr. Debt
Collector, you'd better give me this information so we

can express mail this check to you!" Then send the debt collector the Cease & Desist Letter (Appendix C) via certified mail. See you later! Never pay the debt collector!

MOST PROBABLE NEGATIVE IMPACT OF PAYING THE DEBT COLLECTOR: You've wasted whatever money you've scraped together and opened yourself up for continued harassment at work. You're screwed if you deal with them and you very well may lose your job if you continue to get these harassing phone calls at work. It's against the law, and the cleanest way to take the debt collector out is with written evidence that they have received the Cease & Desist Letter.

SCENARIO #5: You come home from work and there's a note on your front door from one of your neighbors. "Call Vito at (800) 555-1212. Extremely urgent!" You wonder how the debt collector knew to call your neighbor. You feel fear first, then you want to hide. Especially when you talk to the debt collector.

"Hello?"

"Listen, pal. If you don't get that money you owe Rody's Department Store to me by 5:00 this afternoon I'm calling all of your neighbors and telling them that you're nothing more than a deadbeat! You're scum and all of your neighbors are going to know it!"

"How did you know to call my next door neighbor?"

"I know everything about you. I know you owe Crooks Brothers $500 for all of those clothes in your closet. I know you owe Cal-Gas $100 for the gas you've been putting in that '90 Ford you're driving.   I can find you wherever you go! Don't test me. Just pay me!"

REALITY: The debt collector has already (surprise) broken federal law by threatening you with something they **can't** do! It is illegal to discuss your account with any unrelated third party (like your boss, your neighbor, your mother or father, etc.). Furthermore, they've "skip-traced" you. They've used City Directories also known as "Criss-crosses" to contact your neighbors. These directories are readily available at your local library and are another useful tool of terror frequently used by the debt collection industry.

They've also pulled a copy of your credit bureau report and looked down the list of debts you owe. It's not too tough to figure out you spent that $500 for clothes at nationally known Crooks Brothers. It's simple deductive reasoning that let them figure out that the $100 is for gas, and they very easily could have called whomever is financing your car to discreetly find out that make and model car you are buying.

Relax. They're using their tools to do what they do best and intimidate you. But there's a way out.

THE "DOVER-SMART" CONSUMER'S SOLUTION: Act terrified and tell the debt collector that your friend/brother/sister is going to write a check for you. They'll send them $100 . . . $200 . . . but you need to get the debt collector's name, their company name, their address, etc. Tell them that you're borrowing the money and you've got to do what the person lending you the money tells you. "So if you want the money, Mr. Debt Collector, you'd better give me this information so we can express mail this check to you!" Then send the debt collector the Cease & Desist Letter (Appendix C) via certified mail. See you later! Never pay the debt collector!

MOST PROBABLE NEGATIVE IMPACT OF REPAYING THE DEBT COLLECTOR: You've wasted whatever money you've scraped together and opened yourself up for continued harassment of your neighbors at home. You're screwed if you deal with them and you very well may lose any sanity you have remaining if you allow these harassing and intimidating calls to your neighbors to continue. It's against the law for them to discuss your situation with any unrelated third party, including your neighbors, and the cleanest way to take the debt collector out is with written evidence that they have received the Cease & Desist Letter.

Do debt collectors misrepresent themselves?

You draw your own conclusions. Thousands of complaints have been filed against the debt collection industry at state and federal levels for illegal activities like the ones illustrated in the previous pages. There are estimates that for every one complaint actually filed there are at least one thousand incidents that go unreported due to lack of education about these very laws enacted to protect consumers.

Don't ever forget the universal motivation of every debt collector across the country.

GREED.

5

YOU DON'T THINK THEY'D LIE, DO YOU?
THE REAL LOWDOWN ON CONSUMER CREDIT COUNSELING SERVICE

"It is always the best policy to speak the truth, unless, of course, you are an exceptionally good liar."
Jerome K. Jerome

Is it just me or does anybody else out there get the least bit suspicious with all of this Consumer Credit Counseling Service (CCCS) hype?

Have you noticed on the bottom of your consumer credit report that there is a promotional/informational paragraph that touts the many wonders of CCCS? I want to know what they mean when they call CCCS a national, nonprofit association. I have been told that CCCS offices are sold like franchises around the country. They enjoy a brisk business helping consumers wade through their mess of debt, *but at what price?*

I asked Stephen Gardner, a former assistant Attorney General for the State of Texas and the man who initiated the lawsuit against TRW in 1991, about CCCS. His response:

"I think that Consumer Credit Counseling Service is intrinsically deceptive. They're funded or incorporated by the very people they're truly representing . . . not the consumer/debtor but the creditors

trying to collect the money.

"I think they're a con; they pitch themselves as serving the consumer's best interest but they don't. Their promotions practices are deceptive and the consumers are being grossly misled.

"If they were lawyers, they'd get disbarred! Representing one party and acting for the other? Come on! Think about it! If lawyers won't get involved in an enterprise like Consumer Credit Counseling, you *know* it must be bad."

Mr. Gardner's assessment of CCCS fits the picture that became clear while researching this book. Something that the good people at CCCS don't tell you is that they are paid by the creditors. That's right, the very people you owe money to are paying CCCS for the privilege of "helping" you through your debt problems. Isn't that sort of like the having the fox guard the henhouse?

Here's an example:

Suppose you owe Rody's Department Store (among others) $1000, and CCCS assists you in negotiating a repayment schedule to your creditors. You are successful in repaying the entire $1000 through CCCS but in fact, only $875 is returned to the original creditor. A commission equal to 12.5% (in this case $125) is kept by CCCS for "helping" you through this period. *So whose interest is CCCS representing?* The consumer's or the creditor's? Who is paying whom?

If you ask CCCS how they are paid, they will vaguely tell you that they receive a small fee from consumers, plus some funding from local banks and merchants. What they don't tell you is how that funding is derived, i.e., through commissions on the accounts they're servicing.

Furthermore, any notation on your credit bureau reports showing that your account is being handled is far from favorable in the eyes of prospective lenders. What it tells a prospective lender is that you can't handle your debts.

In theory, CCCS is a good idea. Helping consumers repay their bills is wonderful . . . anything to keep them out of bankruptcy court. In addition, CCCS does have a terrific consumer education program that I wish high schools across the nation would add to their curriculum. (What a novel idea . . . teaching consumers how to avoid mistakes before they make them!)

The problem is that CCCS does not make full disclosure to the consumer regarding how CCCS receives remuneration. In addition, in my opinion their reporting on your credit bureau report is a breach of your rights to privacy. Many prospective lenders look at a CCCS notation as favorably as a Chapter 13 (bankruptcy wage-earner plan) filing.

CCCS doesn't have nice offices, extensive staffs, newspaper display advertising and radio/TV commercials, because they're supposedly nonprofit. However, they generate quite a bit of cash for their owners; moreover, creditors love them because they only have to pay a 12.5% commission to CCCS as opposed to as much as 50% to Vito's Knee Breaker Collection Agency.

It's a well-known fact that many credit-card issuers are more willing to accept repayment plans negotiated by Consumer Credit Counseling Service, according to their parent organization, the National Foundation for Consumer Credit. Why? Because as I mentioned previously, they're only paying a 12.5-15% commission instead of up to 50% commission to Vito's Collection Agency. If credit-card issuers are willing to extend these terms through CCCS, why won't they extend them to you or me individually? Something smells here.

Chase Manhattan rejected more than 30% of the repayment plans proposed by CCCS several years ago because they were thought to be overly favorable to debtors. Now, Chase is accepting almost all of these CCCS-originated workout proposals.

Why won't Chase and creditors like them deal with you and me on the same basis?

<u>By the way</u>: I've talked to many, many consumers over the last 18 months who tried to work with CCCS and were rejected. CCCS suggested they file for bankruptcy. Wait a minute! I thought CCCS was there to help consumers *avoid* bankruptcy court. Oh well . . . another one bites the dust.

My advice to you? Play hardball with your creditors and negotiate on your own behalf instead of relying on a third-party (with questionable loyalties) like CCCS to do it for you.

6

SECURED VS. UNSECURED CREDITORS

"A problem well stated is a problem half solved."
Charles F. Kettering

Leverage is what you make of it.

By that I simply mean that as long as you have the upper hand in any negotiation you should consider using it while you've got it, because you can bet the other side always will.

In the majority of cases that involve debtors and debt collectors, most of the debts owed are unsecured.

Like credit card debts. Hospital or medical bills. Or student loans.

Unlike the first two examples of unsecured debts, student loans have risen in the hierarchy of debts to a new status, courtesy of Congress and the IRS. You'll never get out of your student loan debt, so start working towards re-establishing yourself as a fruitful, active consumer repaying your debt to society. Otherwise, the IRS will see you later. (Good news about working out your student loans is in the next chapter.)

Credit cards and medical bills are a different breed. They're almost never secured, making them *un*secured and the #1 source of headaches for not just consumers, but for the original creditors and their team of debt collectors.

I'm not really interested in how you got yourself into the mess you're in . . . just getting you out of it. That's why you need to understand the difference between secured and unsecured creditors.

UNSECURED CREDITORS: THERE'S A REASON WHY THEY CHARGE MORE

Unsecured creditors are always the biggest losers when consumers hit tough financial times. They're usually the last to get paid because they don't have a "secured" position, which means they have nothing more than your signature and promise of repayment as their security. Credit card companies are almost always unsecured, which means they have a larger risk of doing business than other lenders. However, this higher risk allows them to charge higher interest rates—which they have done, historically, with no remorse. At rates as high as 18-21.9%, the credit card industry has a pretty good buffer built in to guard them from potential debtor defaults. When you consider that their cost of funds the last couple of years has been around 4-6%, it all adds up to huge profits on the money they loan through credit cards . . . to the tune of 14-18% on their money. Even when you take defaults into consideration, the major credit card companies are routinely making hundreds of millions of dollars in profits every year!

I'm not telling you this to make you feel any better about not paying your bills. But let's face it: Citibank, Chase Manhattan, Discover and American Express all have this inherent risk when doing business. They all stand to make large profits or take large losses. Fortunately for everyone, their losses have never threatened the future of their companies and are relatively small, less than 3-6% of their outstanding loans. As of June '94 Chase Manhattan Bank reported that 5.6% or $543 million of their $9.6-billion portfolio was more than 60 days past due. It's in their best interest to work aggressively to try to keep these loans from totally defaulting, and the only way they're going to accomplish this is by working with debtors when they're having problems. Otherwise they're not going to get much if it ever does go to bankruptcy court. They may not get much anyway: Even if a consumer never files for bankruptcy, original creditors like Chase know they're not going to see any of their money again if the debtor goes underground. What good is a judgment going to be if you can never collect on it? Lawyers don't get paid for getting judgments, they get paid for recovering money for their client. Everyone is better served if a deal is worked out. (More about this in Chapter 11, "Creative Workouts.") Let's just say at this point that you, the consumer, have the leverage in an unsecured debt situation.

SECURED CREDITORS: DON'T PLAY CAT AND MOUSE

You thought you could make those payments for that brand new sports car.

I know. You loved the smell of the new leather interior. The stereo system was better than most people have in their homes. You couldn't wait to go for a drive. Anywhere. Even driving to work was fun.

But then reality set in. You got a couple of speeding tickets. Your insurance company raised your rates. Maintaining the car cost more than you expected. You can't afford to keep up the payments. You're in deep doo-doo. Now what?

You shrewdly took at least a 20% hit on the value of the car the minute you drove it off the lot. The car dealer isn't interested in making any deals. He's got his money . . . the last thing he needs is another used car. The lease company has just informed you that you've got only 47 payments left on your 60-month lease at $303 per payment. Great. Only $14,000 left on your lease on a car that's worth only $11,000! Now what?

Don't play cat and mouse. Don't hide the car in a friend's garage. Don't look through the blinds when someone knocks on your door late in the evening. Don't delay the inevitable.

Set up an alternate transportation plan. If that means buying a beat-up used car that might not be pretty but runs decently, then go get it. If it means working out a ride every day with a friend or neighbor, than start scheming. If it means having to rely on public transportation, then so be it.

But get covered so you can get to work, to the grocery store, and to your kids, and end the madness.

Call the dealer (if he's financing the car). Call the lease company (if you're leasing the car). Call the finance company (if you're buying the car). Get it over with.

Get all of your possessions out of the car. Write down the mileage. You may even want to take a few pictures of it. You never know if you'll need these later on. Call whomever has the lien on the car and tell them to come pick it up. Or better yet, find out where you can drop it off.

Get a signed receipt from whomever takes the car from you (whether it's the repo man or a representative for the actual lienholder) noting the time that you turned over possession of the car.

MAYBE THERE'S MONEY COMING BACK TO YOU!

If you've been properly insuring the vehicle, call your insurance agent as soon as you can after you've turned the car over and request a refund of any unused premium that you may have paid on the car. After all, why should you insure a car you no longer own? Furthermore, this money will most definitely come in handy if you're having financial problems. It could be 3 months of bus fare. Gas money to give to whomever is giving you rides. Maybe a down payment on a new car from a "tote-the-note" car lot. It's money you're owed, so go get it!

A voluntary repossession (which is what you did when you called the lienholder to come pick up your car because you couldn't pay for it anymore) isn't going to look any better on your credit report that a regular, run-of-the-mill repo. But you'll feel better. You'll know that's one more person you DON'T have to worry about. You won't go out to your parking space after work or in the morning with that sick feeling at the bottom of your stomach. That sick feeling of uncertainty . . . wondering if your car is still there or if they've taken it away, yet. Don't think you'll be able to hide it and keep using it forever. These repo guys are good. They'll always get your car. Don't test them, they'll always win.

YOU CAN'T HIDE YOUR HOUSE

The same goes for your house.

It, too, is a secured asset. The lienholder (the bank or the savings & loan or whoever now owns the note on the house) is in a secured position. If you fail to pay, they get their property back. However, in many cases you have a little more leverage.

Sure, I know. You can't hide a house. They can find you pretty easily, and post a foreclosure notice on your door. Take you down pretty quick and get their property back.

Once again, this is a situation that needs a little more examination.

Do you have equity in your house? Can you price it right and move it quick to get the cash out? Maybe you're in the same position as thousands, perhaps millions of Americans who own a house that's worth less now than when you bought it. (Ever owned a condominium in Texas?)

If you owe more than the property is worth, there's no

digging out anytime soon. If you're behind on your payments, there's probably a slim chance of catching up. The inevitable foreclosure is on the horizon. How far out there is it? How long will it take them to foreclose? Good questions.

I've seen mortgage lienholders foreclose quickly and move former owners out at the earliest possible moment. This happens in probably 20-30% of the cases. I've also seen mortgage companies delay foreclosing for months. Three months . . . six months . . . nine months . . . nothing surprises me.

I've seen them get the foreclosure and not push residents out for months. Many times it depends on how many properties they've got in their problem portfolio. Sometimes the amount of the house or the foreclosure isn't that large. The house might be located in an area that is "less than desirable" and the lienholder knows it's not going to sell anytime soon.

It's time to deal, folks!

DON'T BE AFRAID OF REJECTION!

We all know that (within reason) a house that is being occupied sells easier than an empty house. Unless, of course, the resident has trashed the place and it's value is declining by the minute.

If you're a reasonable soon-to-be-former homeowner who's about to lose your home to foreclosure, it's time to try to cut a deal with the lienholder.

Explain that you cannot pay anymore on your home.

Tell them you are willing to "deed in lieu of foreclosure," which means that instead of the heartache of losing your house on the courthouse steps you're willing to deed the property back over to them. Some lienholders' attorneys/legal departments may still require them to foreclose in order to keep the title clear, but the bottom line here is that you've got a deal for them. Tell them that you can't afford the house payment, which included your taxes and insurance, but that you can afford half. You're willing to stay there and maintain the property, but now as a renter, not as a homeowner. Agree to show the property to potential buyers. Maybe work out a deal that pays you a commission if you bring a buyer to the table (be prepared for them to take whatever that commission is to offset any monies you owe them on your defaulted mortgage), but try to work out a deal. Remember, a house that's lived in looks more like a home, *and homes sell better than houses.*

It's easier to stay put where you are while you're looking for another place to live. It's easier than uprooting the kids from school, or maybe being forced to change schools. The lienholder is deriving some income from the house instead of it just sitting there empty. Everybody wins in a bad situation.

All you've got to do is ask. Give it a try—all they can say is no. If you don't have the guts to go face-to-face with the lienholder or their representative, use the telephone. If you're still too scared to talk on the phone about this, put it in a letter. But get after it. Be aggressive. Stay on the offensive. Just because you've had some hard times financially doesn't make you any less of a good person. Bad things happen to good people. But don't give up without trying. You'd be surprised how often something can be worked out in a bleak situation.

Trust me. I know. I've been in a few.

Give 'em hell!

7

STUDENT LOANS: THEY *WILL* GET YOU!

Argghhh!

Remember when you signed on the dotted line for that cheap money so you could go to college? You had a good time . . . you even fit 4 years of college into 6 years! Hey, it was cheap money, you learned enough to get your degree, and you made friends who will last a lifetime, right?

If you don't take repayment of your student loan seriously, paying for that opportunity to make those friends and have a 6-year party could last a lifetime.

Under the Bush administration, the federal government received authorization to begin offsetting federal income tax refunds for defaulted student loans. You know they're serious when the government can start garnishing your paycheck for non-payment in a state like Texas. Texas has the most protective laws on the books designed to insulate debtors from creditors.

Yet even Texas residents can now feel the wrath of the Department of Education's efforts to recover more than $15 billion in defaulted student loans.

Consider these facts from the Department of Education:

- Student loans are the third most profitable type of lending, beating out both car loans and mortgages.
- Most loans are "risk free" to the lenders, since the government guarantees repayment.
- Since the government guarantees repayment, few lenders put any effort into collecting them.
- If a borrower defaults the government makes good on the loan, plus interest, and the lender avoids the expense of servicing the loan.

Where's the incentive for lenders to screen properly to make the loan, or to make any concerted efforts to collect it?

YOU PLAYED. YOU PAY.

If you played, you've got to pay. That's the bottom line here. However, there are some extenuating circumstances that need to be addressed:

a) With the "easy money" available to young adults from the various federal and state loan programs, a number of scams surfaced. Vocational schools promised young adults qualified training and easy job placement after course completion. In a number of cases, these schools were complete frauds that never delivered on promises, and students were left in debt with nothing to show for their efforts except a stream of debt collection notices and a credit nightmare that won't go away. Finally there's good news! If you can prove that you were deceived or defrauded by the institution, and misled about what they would deliver after you completed the course study, the Department of Education wants to hear from you! There's a way out, but you've got to contact the Department of Education at once.

b) How many young adults right out of high school know anything about debt and credit? How many young adults balance their checkbook? (For that matter, how many older Americans balance their checkbook?) Yet we're allowing 18-year-olds to sign their life away without understanding the full ramifications of their signature on those documents.

c) So now it's time to repay the lender the money they are RIGHTFULLY OWED. Nine months out of school and no job? Too bad. Those monthly invoices start piling up. What do you do? You owe the money, but with your entry level position, you can barely make ends meet. Good news! Thanks to Public Law 103-66, the Student Loan Reform Act, there are a variety of ways that students can avoid the headaches associated with being unable to handle high student loan payments. From Alternative Repayment Plans to Income Contingent Repayment Plans that base the payment amount on the borrower's Adjusted Gross Income, now there's a light at the end of the tunnel— and it's not a train anymore.

d) Maybe you've already joined millions of other Americans and defaulted on your student loan. Did you read the fine print on those loan documents you signed 5 years ago? I didn't think so. Many student loan agreements include provisions for the lender to add an additional 43% to your balance owed if the account goes to a debt collector. Forty-three percent! This is starting to make the loan sharks sound good now. How can you ever pay this debt off? Contact the Department of Education and get ready for some good news.

SOME POSITIVE SOLUTIONS
CONGRESS HAS FINALLY ENACTED

Thanks to the Clinton Administration's efforts, the Student Loan Reform Act became operational on July 1, 1994. Some of the benefits of these reforms include:

1) Tighter regulations for student loans for non-traditional institutions of higher learning. There are some fine vocational institutions out there, but there are some outright scams floating around that spoil it for everyone. These are finally being controlled. The federal government is now making these non-traditional secondary education institutions adhere to reasonable but stringent guidelines for students to qualify for financial assistance.

2) In the reformed repayment program, there are now provisions that allow students enrolled in a school that becomes insolvent to be relieved from their obligation.

3) Thanks to direct lending programs created by these reforms, the cost of these loans will be reduced. The borrower's ability to contact a central clearing house

to discuss all aspects of their debt is now being created. The ability to restructure debts into a variety of repayment plans, with some payouts now extended as long as 30 years, should take even more pressure off not only yesterday's but tomorrow's students.

4) Defaulted student loans now in the hands of debt collectors can be renegotiated to new, attainable terms. Once the borrower has eliminated the third party debt collector as outlined in this book, they may take advantage of new provisions to allow the re-reporting of these loans after the timely repayment of their student loan over a 12 month period allows borrowers to get back on their feet, re-enter the student loan repayment system and not be penalized for years to come.

HERE ARE SOME ADDITIONAL IMPROVEMENTS I'D LIKE TO SEE

Our lawmakers finally got it right with these reforms. I'd still like to see some additional improvements to the student loan system that would include the following:

1) Require every student coming out of high school to pass a basic consumer literacy test. I'm not trying to make Harvard MBAs out of high school graduates, but I believe that today's graduates of either high school or college are woefully under prepared for the simplest form of finance: balancing a checkbook. Keep it simple, but make sure students understand what a debt obligation is and how it will affect them over the long haul.

2) Require every student borrower to watch a 15-

minute video presentation explaining the document they are about to sign and their obligation to repay all monies borrowed. Make sure they understand that this is a debt they must honor, and don't allow borrowers to rush them through the fine print. Student borrowers have got to understand what they're signing.

3) President Clinton has proposed a government jobs program that will allow student loan borrowers/graduates to work off their obligation. Many states have similar programs in operation, allowing borrowers to work off their debt if they become teachers, for example. In short, certain job arenas excuse student debt. This is a good idea and a viable solution to the current crisis of defaulted loans.

4) Quit reimbursing lenders 100% for defaulted student loans. How about 50%? Okay, 75% reimbursement on defaulted loans is reasonable. I promise you the lenders won't be making as many flaky loans as they have been in the past.

5) Finally, allow the interest on student loans to be deductible, like home mortgage interest. Getting a post-secondary education in the 1990s is an expensive proposition, especially if an MBA, a law degree or the granddaddy of them all, a medical degree, is the goal. Balances exceeding $100,000 aren't unusual anymore, so let's give tomorrow's leaders and professionals a fighting chance.

Since 1986 the U.S. Department of Education has forwarded over 10 million names and corresponding account information to the IRS to withhold tax refunds and pay off a portion of the student loan debt.

In 1992, for example, the IRS withheld 720,326 refunds, representing $530 million in student loan repayments. Since 1986 the IRS has offset 3,225,039 tax refunds, repaying over $2.1 billion in defaulted student loans.

By the way, don't feel bad. You're not alone. According to a General Accounting Office report last year, hundreds of IRS employees had delinquent non-tax government debts such as students loans and child support payments. I wonder if they're offsetting their own tax refund checks? Hmmmm. Just a thought.

DEFAULTED STUDENT LOAN SOLUTIONS FOR TODAY'S CONSUMERS

Step 1: If you are being harassed by a debt collector about your student loan, take them out immediately. Use the strategies outlined in this book to accomplish this goal. By eliminating the debt collector from the collection loop you will be able to deal with the original lender, or current note holder or loan servicer.

Step 2: Don't let the loan get all the way to the IRS stage. Negotiate, negotiate, negotiate. You must communicate with the lender/servicer first and try to obtain a deferment. Some lenders will allow up to 3 years, giving you ample time to get on your feet. These deferments will stop interest expense from accruing and keep consumers from being buried when they restart their repayment. Incidentally, borrowers have over a dozen deferment categories to qualify under, ranging from inability to finding employment, poor health, service in the military or Peace Corps, or a desire to go back to school (and run up higher student loan balances!).

Step 3: Investigate the possibility of getting a student loan consolidation loan. This will extend the time it will take to repay your loan, but will allow you the chance to possibly lower your interest rate and your payments, and most importantly, save your credit rating. A loan consolidator that fits into this category is Nellie Mae (New England Education Loan Marketing Corporation) at (800) 338-5626. If they cannot help you they may be able to refer you to someone in your part of the country.

Step 4: If you know your loan is in default, make the first move; contact the Department of Education at (800) 433-3243 and ask for their Credit Management and Debt Collection Services unit. Explain your situation, keep detailed notes of people you talk to and when, and then follow up with a letter confirming your discussions. Be sure to send this letter via certified mail so there are no mistakes. Use the letter in Appendix G as your suggested model for correspondence.

Step 5: If you have to deal with negative impact on your credit bureau report from defaulting on a student loan used to attend one of these "questionable" vocational institutions, consider disputing this transaction with the credit bureaus. Get your hands on a copy of *LIFE AFTER DEBT:* **The Blueprint For Surviving**

In America's Credit Society by (you guessed it) Benjamin Dover and go after the credit bureaus!

Step 6: Write to the Department of Education in Washington, D.C. and tell them you need help! They really do want to see borrowers get back into the system without too much brain damage. They are finally allowed to recognize that student loan borrowers who are allowed to work back into the system are not only grateful, but also a positive impact on the national economy. The Department of Education will now reclassify your defaulted student loan as current if you successfully make 12 consecutive payments. A second chance on your credit report? Yes!

Address your correspondence to:

U.S. Department of Education
7th & D Streets, Room 5102
Washington, D.C. 20202

Remember, *you have rights.* Senate investigations led by Senator Sam Nunn [D-Ga.] revealed lenders that failed to adhere to Department of Education guidelines. Surprise.

The Department of Education has failed to supervise over 10,000 primary lenders and 64 institutions operating in the secondary educational loan market. There are indications that 8 out of 10 lenders were not following proper DOE collection guidelines/procedures. Surprise.

THIRTY-YEAR STUDENT LOAN REPAYMENT PERIODS? A MAJOR BREAKTHROUGH!

As mentioned earlier in this chapter, the government has finally acknowledged that many student loan balances rival home mortgage balances in amount owed the lender, and has now created repayment schedules that extend up to 30 years.

Direct lending is planned to be available through 104 schools during the first year of the new and innovative higher education financing program resulting from the Student Loan Reform Act enacted in August, 1993. "Direct lending is user-friendly; the program makes borrowing simpler and more affordable," says Richard W. Riley, U.S. Secretary of Education. "This clearly marks a major milestone in reforming financial aid programs for students."

Approximately $1 billion in direct loans, or 5% of the total student loan volume, will be made at 104 schools during the program's inaugural year, 1994-95. By academic year 1998-99 direct loans will comprise at least 60% of total volume.

Most importantly, students with other types of federal student loans may consolidate the loans and take advantage of a range of repayment options, including a plan tailored to the borrowers' income . . . for a change.

Thanks to the Student Reform Act, students will now be able to receive loans through their schools and bypass private lenders. As a result of these and other changes, taxpayers should be saved an estimated $4.3 billion over five years.

In addition, students with balances of $60,000 or more will be able to choose a 30-year repayment term, or choose to make a fixed monthly payment for 10 years, with another payment for an additional 12-30 years. Another option planned to be offered will allow the loan to be paid for 12 to 30 years at a monthly rate that varies with the loan balance, or monthly payments based on a percentage of income for up to 25 years.

Any way you look at it, our lawmakers and the Department of Education are finally waking up to the fact that yesterday's students sometimes need a fraction of the leniency that we extended to Chrysler back in the late 1970s when they were experiencing difficult times financially.

Compassion from our government? Legislators responding to our needs without the enticement of major campaign contributions? *What's going on here?*

Take advantage of these programs before they change their minds! And make every penny count. After all, you could be paying it back for the next 30 years!

8

UNDERSTANDING THE FAIR DEBT COLLECTION PRACTICES ACT

*"If you don't know where you are going,
every road will get you nowhere."*
Henry Kissinger

If you're like me, you probably wonder what our law-makers in Washington do besides raise taxes and spend too much of our hard-earned tax dollars. The laws they enact seem to protect the wrong people if they have any teeth or enforceability at all . . . except in one case. The debt collection industry vs. you and me—the average American consumer.

It sure must have been bad back in the 1970s. The debt collection industry must have really been vicious—even more heartless than they are today—to get our legislators off their rears and putting laws on the books that related to everyone, especially those suffering through difficult financial times.

The Fair Debt Collection Practices Act became Public Law 95-108 on September 20, 1977 and was updated/amended by Public Law 99-361 on July 9, 1986. This law is probably the most powerful, yet least understood or utilized consumer protection law ever . . . until 1992, when I started educating consumers about their rights in dealing with debt collectors.

It's complicated, like any piece of legislation that becomes federal law. That's why I've written this book. To help you learn about this law, how to use it and benefit from the protection it provides all of us. Once you learn what it all means you'll be well on your way to getting back on your feet.

I'm going to break down the most important sections of the law (there's a full reprint of the entire law in Appendix L in the back of this book) and explain clearly what it means to you and me.

(NOTE: There are so many points to this law, I will clarify/restate them in smaller groups so it's easier for you to digest and hopefully, understand.)

§804. Acquisition of Location Information

Any debt collector communicating with any person other than the consumer for the purpose of acquiring location information about the consumer shall—

1) Identify himself, state that he is confirming or correcting location information concerning the consumer, and, only if expressly requested, identify his employer;

2) Not state that the consumer owes any debt;

3) Not communicate with any such person more than once unless requested to do so by such person or unless the debt collector reasonably believes that the earlier response of such person is erroneous or incomplete and that such person now has correct or complete location information;

4) Not communicate by postcard;

5) Not use any language or symbol on the envelope or in the contents of any communication effected by the mails or telegram that indicates that the debt collector is in the debt collection business or that the communication is related to the collection of a debt; and

6) After the debt collector knows the consumer is represented by an attorney with regard to the subject debt and has knowledge of, or can readily ascertain, such attorney's name and address, not communicate with any person other than that attorney, unless the attorney fails to respond within a reasonable period of time to communication from the debt collector.

IN PLAIN ENGLISH:

When the debt collector is trying to find you they can't . . .

1) Tell everyone that they're debt collectors out looking for you;

2) Tell anyone that you owe money;

3) Contact your family, friends, neighbors, etc. more than once while trying to find you, unless they think that person has intentionally given bad information out about you;

4) Use a postcard (Think about it! Wouldn't they love to use it if they could, in order to embarrass you?);

5) Send you a letter with the return address showing it's from a collection agency;

6) Keep calling people to "look" for you after they know that you're being represented by an attorney. This part of the law hopefully restrains the debt collectors

from intimidating you by making repeated contacts with your family, friends, neighbors, etc. Be aware that many times, this does not stop them from these tactics, so be sure to keep track of all contacts the debt collector makes to others (where possible without self-inflicted embarrassment).

§805. Communication In Connection With Debt Collection

Communication with the consumer generally—
Without the prior consent of the consumer given directly to the debt collector, or the express permission of a court of competent jurisdiction, a debt collector may not communicate with a consumer in connection with the collection of any debt—

1) At any usual time or place or a time or place known or which should be known to be inconvenient to the consumer. In the absence of knowledge of circumstances to the contrary, a debt collector shall assume that the convenient time for communicating with a consumer is after 8:00 a.m. and before 9:00 p.m. local time at the consumer's location;

2) If the debt collector knows the consumer is represented by an attorney with respect to such debt and has knowledge of, or can readily ascertain, such attorney's name and address, unless the attorney fails to respond within a reasonable period of time to communication from the debt collector or unless the attorney consents *to direct communication with the consumer; or*

3) At the consumer's place of employment if the debt collector knows or has reason to know that the consumer's employer prohibits the consumer from receiving such communication.

IN PLAIN ENGLISH:

1) No "middle-of-the-night wake-up calls" from the debt collector. They are authorized to call you between 8 a.m. and 9 p.m. your local time, not theirs. Don't accept any of these "Oh, I forgot you're in another time zone" excuses. They know better.

2) If the debt collector knows you've got an attorney handling your situation, they've got to contact the attorney. They can't keep calling you.

3) The debt collector can call you at work, unless the debt collector already knows that you can't take calls at work (like from a previous call taken by a supervisor) or if you tell the debt collector clearly: "Look. I can't take calls from you here at work. Don't ever call me here again!" Then hang up. You've put them on notice (but the cleanest way is sending them the Cease & Desist letter located in Appendix C).

Communication with third parties—
Except as provided in section 804, without the prior consent of the consumer given directly to the debt collector, or the express permission of a court of competent jurisdiction, or as reasonable necessary to effectuate a post judgment judicial remedy, a debt collector may not communicate, in connection with the collection of any debt, with any person other than the consumer, his

attorney, a consumer reporting agency if otherwise permitted by law, the creditor, the attorney of the creditor, or the attorney of the debt collector.

IN PLAIN ENGLISH:

The debt collector can't discuss your debt with anyone else except for you, your attorney (if you are using one), or a credit reporting agency. They can't call your boss, your family or your neighbors. If they do they've broken the law. Don't be afraid to go after the debt collector. It's your right if they're breaking federal law.

Ceasing communication—

If a consumer notifies a debt collector in writing that the consumer refuses to pay a debt or that the consumer wishes the debt collector to cease further communication with the consumer, the debt collector shall not communicate further with the consumer with respect to such debt, except-

1) To advise the consumer that the debt collector's further efforts are being terminated;

2) To notify the consumer that the debt collector or creditor may invoke specified remedies which are ordinarily invoked by such debt collector or creditor; or,

3) Where applicable, to notify the consumer that the debt collector or creditor intends to invoke a specified remedy.

If such notice from the consumer is made by mail, notification shall be complete upon receipt.

IN PLAIN ENGLISH:

I keep referring to the Cease & Desist letter throughout this book as being the key to regaining control of your situation. This letter is your "silver bullet" in taking the debt collector out of your life. This section of the law describes that very letter.

Once you've sent the Cease & Desist letter, the debt collector:

1) Can contact you only one more time to advise you that they won't be contacting you (about this particular debt, anyway) anymore;

2) Can tell you that either they plan to, or advise their client (the original creditor) to, in most cases, sue you. This is their right—to sue you, that is. But what the debt collector really hopes to accomplish is to scare you (with the threat of a lawsuit) into paying them what you owe the original creditor. Sorry! We're not going to pay you! Only the original creditor will ever see a penny. Adios, Mr. Debt Collector!

3) Finally, and most important, if you (the consumer) notify the debt collector by mail that you do not plan on dealing with them, notification is deemed completed and they are history. Remember to send this letter by Certified Mail/Return Receipt Requested so you have proof that they received your letter. You don't want to hear any excuses about not getting your letter, do you?

The term "consumer" is meant to include you (the debtor), your spouse, your parents (if you're a minor), your guardian, executor or administrator.

§806. Harassment or abuse

A debt collector may not engage in any conduct the natural consequence of which is to harass, oppress, or abuse any person in connection with the collection of a debt. Without limiting the general application of the foregoing, the following conduct is a violation of this section:

1) The use or threat of use of violence or other criminal means to harm the physical person, reputation or property of any person;

2) The use of obscene or profane language or language the natural consequence of which is to abuse the hearer or reader;

3) The publication of a list of consumers who allegedly refuse to pay debts, except to a consumer reporting agency;

4) The advertisement for sale of any debt to coerce payment of the debt;

5) Causing a telephone to ring or engaging any person in telephone conversation repeatedly or continuously with intent to annoy, abuse, or harass any person at the called number;

6) Except as provided in section 804, the placement of telephone calls without meaningful disclosure of the caller's identity.

IN PLAIN ENGLISH:

1) Obviously, the debt collector cannot threaten to hurt you physically or to destroy your reputation or any property you may own. Amazingly, this is one of the most violated parts of the law—don't let them do it to you! They love to make idle threats but remember, that's just what they are . . . idle threats.

2) Some of these debt collectors could make a sailor blush. They'll attack you with every obscenity in the book

if they think they can scare you into paying them. You know better. (You'll probably want to buy a telephone recording device at Radio Shack, discussed in grater detail in Chapter 10. This can give you hours of fun!)

3) They can't put your name on a list of "deadbeats" and publish it in the paper or post it in public. All they can do is discreetly report you to the credit reporting bureaus.

4) They can't threaten to advertise your debt for sale in order to force you to repay them. Another illegal threat.

5) This one is probably the most frequently violated of all: They can NOT keep calling you on the phone. They can't call and hang up, or let the phone ring and hang up right before you get to it. This is a favorite technique but one that can really hang them if you catch them. And with current developing telephone technology and records, you can catch them!

6) They can't make anonymous phone calls. This is a favorite one for female debt collectors to use to stir things up around the house. A female collector will call and ask for "Bob" and when Bob's wife answers and starts quizzing the debt collector, the collector makes comments that will most certainly get Bob into a fight with his wife. Remember, if you ask a collector "point blank" who they are and what they want, they must tell you. They can't lie or misrepresent their identity. But they'll try. That's why the next part of the law exists. Our lawmakers saw this one coming back in the '70s.

Read on . . . .

§807. False or misleading representations

A debt collector may not use any false, deceptive or misleading representation or means in connection with the collection of any debt. Without limiting the general application of the foregoing, <u>the following conduct is a violation of this section</u>:

1) The false representation or implication that the debt collector is vouched for, bonded by, or affiliated with the United States or any State, including the use of any badge, uniform or facsimile thereof.

2) The false representation of—

(a) the character, amount, or legal status of any debt; or,

(b) any services rendered or compensation which may be lawfully received by any debt collector for the collection of a debt.

3) The false representation or implication that any individual is an attorney or that any communication is from an attorney.

4) The representation or implication that nonpayment of any debt will result in the arrest or imprisonment of any person or the seizure, garnishment, attachment, or sale of any property or wages of any person unless such action is lawful and the debt collector or creditor intends to take such action.

5) The threat to take any action that cannot legally be taken or that is not intended to be taken.

IN PLAIN ENGLISH:

1) The debt collector cannot try to give you the false impression that they're affiliated or connected in any

way with the government (federal or state) by either stating this in a letter or on the phone or even insinuating this. This is a favorite tactic, especially between February and May of each year. Some collectors will tell you that ". . . according to our records (or friends) at the IRS, you are due a sizeable tax refund and had better send it to us!" This is obviously a numbers game—they know millions of Americans receive tax refunds, and it's a blatant attempt to intimidate the consumer into thinking they're "connected" with the IRS. Bull.

2) Many times the debt collector may tell you the debt is for more than it really is, hoping to scare you into agreeing to pay the smaller (actual) amount owed. The collector may also tell you this debt has already gone to trial and you'd better pay up or the judge may add additional fees. The collector may try to convince you that they can or already have added enormous fees that they will collect for their services in collecting the debt. More bull.

3) Another favorite of the debt collector is to tell you that they're calling from the "LEGAL DEPARTMENT" or that the collector is a "paralegal." The collector may be very convincing and use a variety of terms to try to make you believe that you're dealing with someone who is an attorney, when they aren't! Many collection letters may attempt to use letterhead that looks very "official" or as if it's from an attorneys' office. U.S. government logos, eagles and other official-looking seals are favorites of the really stupid debt collectors, who think they're going to scare you into paying their office.

4) Still another favorite. "Sir, you've got until 5 p.m. today to get full payment into our offices or we will have to have the sheriff pick you up." Threats to seize your personal property when they can't are common. Their story is that if they notify the courts that you are an irresponsible deadbeat, the courts may take your children to a foster home since you are probably an unfit parent! Believe me, they'll say whatever works in order to scare you into paying them. Furthermore, in some states (like Texas) it is illegal for a creditor to garnish your paycheck. If a debt collector calling from another state threatens you with an action that is not legal in your state, this is yet another violation of this portion of the law.

5) As I mentioned in the previous paragraph, it's illegal for a debt collector to threaten an action that is not enforceable in your state. Furthermore, if the debt collector is threatening you with actions it could take but has never taken, this too is against the law. If they threaten to do something, they'd better be ready to prove that they have taken this action before.

6) The false representation or implication that a sale, referral, or other transfer of any interest in a debt shall cause the consumer to—

a) lose any claim or defense to payment of the debt; or
b) become subject to any practice prohibited by this title.

7) The false representation or implication that the consumer committed any crime or other conduct in order to disgrace the consumer.

8) Communicating or threatening to communicate to any person credit information which is known or which should be known to be false, including the failure to communicate that a disputed debt is disputed.

9) The use or distribution of any written communication which simulates or is falsely represented to be a document authorized, issued or approved by any court, official, or agency of the United States or any State, or which creates a false impression as to its source, authorization, approval.

10) The use of any false representation or deceptive means to collect or attempt to collect any debt or to obtain information concerning a consumer.

IN PLAIN ENGLISH:

6) Another favorite tactic used to put the heat on consumers. It's illegal for the debt collector to coerce you into repaying them a debt with the threat of losing any defensive position regarding this debt. It's also illegal to threaten to do something that's not allowed by law in your state (such as the threat of garnishing your paycheck, when in a state like Texas it's illegal).

7) Ever heard this line from a debt collector? "It's pretty apparent to us that you used this card knowing that you couldn't repay the debt. That's fraud! You've committed a crime. You can go to jail for that!" Not only is that illegal for the debt collector to say, but it's one of the most frequently used tactics of intimidation.

8) You have a right to dispute any debt that is not correct. It may not be correct for a variety of reasons: Goods or services never received, incorrect amount

being charged, etc. Whatever the case, if you have notified the debt collector (verbally, but best by letter) that
this debt is being disputed, it is illegal for them to report
this to anyone unless they acknowledge that the debt is
in dispute. Furthermore, it's illegal for the debt collector to report ANYTHING that is false . . . and by God,
they'd sure better be able to document anything they
decide to report to the credit bureau, or they've broken
another federal law.

9) A great scare tactic they like to use on unsuspecting
consumers—some of their documents look like either a
court summons or something issued by the Internal
Revenue Service. They'll try just about anything to get
an edge, so scrutinize anything that looks "official"
before getting too scared. Don't forget, these people are
pros at intimidation.

10) This is probably the most frequently violated part
of the law, and the most difficult to prove. Debt collectors will use a variety of stories to find a consumer, such
as: "I'm an old friend . . ." or "I'm his brother/sister . . ."
or "I used to work with him over at . . ." or more creative ones, like: "I'm his insurance agent and we finally
got his claim check in the amount of $550 in today's
mail. Could you have him call me at . . . ?" They're
breaking the law any time they lie to get information
about you.

*11) Except as otherwise provided for, communications
to acquire location information under section 804, the
failure to disclose clearly in all communications made*

to collect a debt or to obtain information about a consumer, that the debt collector is attempting to collect a debt and that any information obtained will be used for that purpose.

12) The false representation or implication that accounts have been turned over to innocent purchasers for value.

13) The false representation or implication that documents are legal process.

14) The use of any business, company, or organization name other than the true name of the debt collector's business, company, or organization.

15) The false representation or implication that documents are not legal process forms or do not require action by the consumer.

16) The false representation or implication that a debt collector operates or is employed by a consumer reporting agency as defined by section 603(f) of this Act.

IN PLAIN ENGLISH:

11) This statement has pretty much become a standard part of any collection letter, and can normally be found at the bottom of the letter. Keep in mind that the debt
collector doesn't have to have this at the bottom of any correspondence and that anything you say, write or let be known will be used against you in your dealings with the debt collector. Remember, "Loose lips sink ships."

12) Another ploy to intimidate you to pay the debt collector—the claim that your account was sold to an innocent party that paid in good faith for your debt.

Don't believe it.

13) Similar to #9 (above), this technique is a favorite scare tactic and is easy to nail the debt collector with since you have undisputable proof of their violation of this part of the law.

14) Another favorite tactic used today—debt collectors love to intimidate! They'll use company names that sound impressive and very legal . . . or very threatening. Smaller, local or regional debt collection agencies like this one. Don't fall for it.

15) Not so common a tactic, but one still occasionally used. The debt collector strategy here is extremely sneaky . . . they lull the consumer into thinking they don't have to reply. The consumer fails to respond in time to an actual court action, and the debt collector or their attorney gets a judgment and the ability to levy on your assets, if you're not careful. Once again, this type of deception is easy to prove but could be costly to pursue since you'd need to hire an attorney to fight your battle in the courts, and money is obviously already tight and a scarce commodity.

16) Let's say a debt collector calls up and says they're trying to collect, and adds, "Oh yeah, by the way—if you don't pay this bill to me and me only I'm afraid I'll have to put this on your credit report through our affiliate company, TransUnion!" If the debt collection agency is not owned and therefore not a part of a consumer reporting agency (credit bureau), then they've violated the law. But let me warn you: CSC/Equifax has increased their foothold in this part of the business

and owns several affiliates that do indeed collect debts and really are a part of the credit bureau system. Once again, you've got to know who you're dealing with. **Always.**

§808. *Unfair practices*

A debt collector may not use unfair or unconscionable means to collect or attempt to collect any debt. Without limiting the general application of the foregoing, the following conduct is a violation of this section:

1) The collection of any amount (including any interest, fee, charges, or expense incidental to the principal obligation) unless such amount is expressly authorized by the agreement creating the debt or permitted by law.

2) The acceptance by a debt collector from any person of a check or other payment instrument postdated by more than five days unless such person is notified in writing of the debt collector's intent to deposit such check or instrument not more than ten nor less than three business days prior to such deposit.

3) The solicitation by a debt collector of any postdated check or other postdated payment instrument for the purpose of threatening or instituting criminal prosecution.

4) Depositing or threatening to deposit any postdated check or other postdated payment instrument prior to the date on such check or instrument.

IN PLAIN ENGLISH:

1) You've got to admire them for trying. Those debt

collectors like to increase their profitability by adding on special collection fees from time to time. They will sometimes add enormous fees to your actual debt and then "settle" for a lesser amount. The fact is that unless the original loan agreement you signed with the original creditor specifies certain monetary penalties for late payment or default, or these are allowed by state law (they're not), then too bad for the debt collector. They simply cannot add on arbitrary fees.

2) A favorite of the debt collection community is getting consumers to send postdated checks. "Hey, you want me to stop the process servers from coming out to your job? I can cancel the lawsuit if you send me twelve postdated checks for $100!" *Wrong!* The debt collector has a responsibility to let you know prior to depositing a postdated check (they rarely do). Furthermore, I know of many instances when a debt collector has deposited checks early, causing them to bounce. Which, in turn, costs the consumer "Non-Sufficient Funds" (overdraft) fees . . . you know the story. It's a nightmare that can easily be avoided. Never send a postdated check to anyone, especially a debt collector. Better yet, and in case you haven't figured it out by now, never deal with a debt collector.

3) Another twist on the previous portion of the law just discussed deals with that recurring theme of intimidation. Many debt collectors sense when a consumer is sending them a postdated check "just to get them off my back." They know that in these cases the chances are usually pretty high that the consumer will bounce a

postdated check. Which is exactly what the debt collector wants. The consumer is then scared by the threats now being hurled through the phone by the debt collector: *"All I've got to do now is turn these checks over to the District Attorney and you won't have to worry about any more calls from me or any other debt collector . . . because you'll be in jail!"* The debt collector knows the fear everybody has (or should have, anyway) of going to jail, and they're quick to capitalize on it. It's illegal, but it should never happen in the first place. Never send a postdated check, period.

4) Another example of holding the consumer's feet to the fire by threatening to deposit those postdated checks early. Sorry, guys! This too, is against the law!

5) Causing charges to be made to any person for communications by concealment of the true purpose of the communication. Such charges include, but are not limited to, collect telephone calls and telegram fees.

6) Taking or threatening to take any nonjudicial action to effect dispossession of property if—

a) there is no present right to possession of the property claimed as collateral through an enforceable security interest;

b) there is no present intention to take possession of the property; or

c) the property is exempt by law from such dispossession or disablement.

7) Communicating with a consumer regarding a debt by post card.

8) Using any language or symbol, other than the debt collector's address, on any envelope when communicating with a consumer by use of mails or by telegram, except that a debt collector may use his business name if such name does not indicate that he is in the debt collection business.

IN PLAIN ENGLISH:

5) Deceptive "collect" calls or telegrams that the consumer ends up paying for is the target of this portion of the law. It doesn't happen much, but everything seems to move in cycles in this business. It could always resurface again later. Don't get stuck paying for anything like that.

6) Yet another favorite of your friendly debt collector—threatening to repossess your car, your boat, your TV set . . . even if they have no security interest in any of these items. Remember, a debt collector is powerless to repossess anything unless they have a lien against it. And they certainly can't repo something over a debt that hasn't yet been settled in a court of law. But they'll never tell you this. They'll just try to scare you into paying on the debt they're trying to collect. This portion of the law also prohibits the debt collector from threatening to repo an item even if they have no intention of doing so—"sabre rattling," I call it. If they haven't done it before they don't have a leg to standon if they try to threaten you with this tactic. By the way, if your local or state law prohibits the debt collector from repossessing or disabling a particular item, the threat of doing this is also against the law.

7) Back in the dark ages of the 1960s and 1970s debt collectors used to send threatening postcards about your debt. No more. That was outlawed in 1977.

8) So was sending letters that were plainly marked as originating from a debt collection agency. All they can put on the return address portion of the envelope is the name of their company, as long as "DEBT COLLEC-TION" is not part of the title. In other words, there can be no language or symbols indicating the letter is from a collection agency.

§809. Validation of debts

Within five days after the initial communication with a consumer in connection with the collection of any debt, a debt collector shall, unless the following information is contained in the initial communication or the consumer has paid the debt, send the consumer a written notice containing—

1) The amount of the debt;

2) The name of the creditor to whom the debt is owed;

3) A statement that unless the consumer, within thirty days after receipt of notice, disputes the validity of the debt, or any portion thereof, the debt will be assumed to be valid by the debt collector;

4) A statement that if the consumer notifies the debt collector in writing within the thirty- day period that the debt, or any portion thereof, is disputed, the debt collector will obtain verification of the debt or a copy of the judgment against the consumer and a copy of such verification or judgment will be mailed to the consumer by the debt collector.

IN PLAIN ENGLISH:

1 & 2) Should be pretty straightforward.

3) All this means is that unless you notify the debt collector in writing (always put everything in writing!) that it is an invalid or disputed debt, the debt collector can only assume that the debt is valid and will pursue you.

4) Your first love letter from your "friendly" debt collector must contain this statement, which lets you know that they will pursue the collection of the debt unless you dispute it, in writing, within thirty days from the date of their letter. Wake up! Are you listening? The only letter you need to send to the debt collector is a Cease & Desist Letter. Whether you owe the debt or not, don't deal with the debt collector. (There is a special Cease & Desist letter format in Appendix C in the back of this book that you can use for debts that you ARE disputing, and which also serves as their notice to buzz off.)

5) A statement that, upon the consumer's written request within the thirty day period, the debt collector will provide the consumer with the name and address of the original creditor, if different from the current creditor;

6) If the consumer notifies the debt collector in writing within the thirty day period described that the debt, or any portion thereof, is disputed, or that the consumer requests the name and address of the original creditor, the debt collector shall cease collection of the debt, or any disputed portion thereof, until the debt collector obtains verification of the debt or a copy of the judgment, or the name and address of the original creditor, and a copy of such verification or judgment, or name and address of the original creditor, is mailed to the consumer by the debt collector;

7) Failure of a consumer to dispute the validity of a debt under this section may not be construed by any court as an admission of liability by the consumer.

IN PLAIN ENGLISH:

5) You have the right to know the name and address of the original creditor if you notify the debt collector that you are requesting this, once again within thirty days.

6) If you do notify the debt collector that you are disputing the debt, or any portion of the debt, then the debt collector must immediately cease any and all collection efforts until they verify that the debt they are trying to collect is valid. The debt collector must also mail you a copy of the confirmation/verification of the debt or judgment.

7) Even if you, the consumer, fail to notify the debt collector within the thirty-day period that you are disputing the validity of part or all the debt in question, this may not be interpreted by any court that you admit to owing the debt. Don't let a debt collector try to convince you that you lose because you didn't notify them in time. Remember Dover's Rule in case you haven't figured it out by now: <u>Never deal with the debt collector!</u>

§810. Multiple debts

If any consumer owes multiple debts and makes any single payment to any debt collector with respect to such debts, such debt collector may not apply such payment to any debt which is disputed by the consumer and, where applicable, shall apply such payment in accordance with the consumer's directions.

IN PLAIN ENGLISH:

Let's say you've got a regular revolving account/credit line with a department store and also an account reserved for large purchases, like fine jewelry, appliances, etc. You have a dispute with the store over something on your revolving account and they assign it to a debt collector.

In the meantime, they turn your other account over to the debt collector because now you're on their bad list and they've decided to cut you off. You continue to pay on the other account for the large purchase that you made because you have no dispute over this account or amount. You send in your regular payment to the debt collector and tell them to apply it to the account that is correct and they apply it to the disputed account. They've violated federal law!

A debt collector <u>must</u> apply the money to the account you instruct them to (always in writing . . . make a note where you want it credited on the "memo" line on the bottom left of your check).

Better yet—<u>don't</u> deal with the debt collector and you won't have this problem.

§811. Legal actions by debt collectors

Any debt collector who brings any legal action on a debt against any consumer shall—

1) In the case of an action to enforce an interest in real property securing the consumer's obligation, bring such action only in a judicial district or similar legal entity in which such real property is located; or

2) In the case of an action not described (in the previous paragraph) bring such action only in the judicial district or similar legal entity—

a) In which such consumer signed the contract sued upon; or

b) In which such consumer resides at the commencement of the action.

3) Nothing in this title shall be construed to authorize the bringing of legal actions by debt collectors.

IN PLAIN ENGLISH:

1) Let's assume the debt collector is suing you over $1,000 you owe on a stereo system. Suppose you live in Los Angeles and the debt collector is located in New York. The debt collector cannot cause a lawsuit to be filed against you in New York. They must sue you where the property (the stereo system, in this instance) is located, which is probably with you in Los Angeles, right?

2) They've got to sue you on your home turf, or where you last lived when they filed the lawsuit. Fair is fair . . . the debt collector can't be expected to chase you all over the country if you are purposely trying to evade your creditors.

3) Nothing in this law may be misinterpreted as a license for debt collectors to file lawsuits. Sorry, guys!

§812. Furnishing certain deceptive forms

1) It is unlawful to design, compile and furnish any form knowing that such form would be used to create the false belief in a consumer that a person other than the creditor of such consumer is partici- pating in the collection of or in an attempt to collect a debt such consumer allegedly owes such creditor, when in fact such person is not so participating.

2) Any person who violates this section shall be liable to the same extent and the same manner as a debt collector is liable under section 813 for failure to comply with a provision of this title.

IN PLAIN ENGLISH:

1) Another favorite technique, the use of which runs in cycles . . . the creation of a separate "paper" company that is now supposedly assisting or even exclusively handling the collection of a debt. Once again, these wonderful debt collectors will try just about anything to reach their goal of squeezing money out of you, and that includes creating ominous companies that will intimi- date you into writing them a check. Don't fall for it. Besides, it's illegal!

2) This means anyone caught playing these reindeer games will get their hand slapped like any other run-of- the-mill debt collector, as outlined in the civil liability

portion of this law.

§813. Civil liability

This section, and the remainder of this law, is more "legalese" that sounds impressive but is rarely utilized. If you're really interested in this portion of the Fair Debt Collection Practices Act, refer to Appendix L starting on page 199. But it's not that valuable to you, the consumer.

Unfortunately, few debt collection agencies are ever pursued by civil lawsuit filed by consumers. But many have been sued by the Federal Trade Commission or the Attorney Generals of states across the nation. So if you are harassed by a debt collector using some of these illegal tricks, let your tax dollars work for you and go after them. You're armed with enough knowledge to set the trap and document their violations.

Few civil attorneys will pursue this type of litigation on a contingency basis because they're simply not familiar with the laws, but the FTC and AG's offices will. You don't have to take any abuse from debt collectors!

Remember, take them out early with the Cease & Desist letter. Then, if they persist, drop them into the laps of the authorities. If you don't, it will only get worse.

9

COVERING YOUR ASSETS

*"The will to persevere in the face of obstacles
is often the difference between
success and failure."*
Anonymous

The biggest battle when you've gone to war with your creditors, their "hired gun" debt collector, or even an attorney retained to sue you is between your ears. Overcoming the fear of being sued and the fear of being pursued.

It's an awful feeling when the phone rings and you're afraid to answer it.

It's a terrible feeling to be afraid to go to your mailbox or answer the knock of the postal carrier at your front door.

So why should you be such a *target*?

Why be so easy to find . . . so accommodating to your opposition? The answer is simple enough.

You don't have to be. Insulate yourself from the debt collectors and you're more than halfway home on your journey back from creditor hell. Get invisible. Make it hard for them to find you. To a degree and for awhile, go underground. Read on and find out how.

MAIL DROPS, ANYONE?

STEP ONE: Go to the nearest post office and get yourself a post office box. Sometimes a better alternative is to call on the services of a commercial mail drop service such as Mailboxes, Etc. and create a new address in a matter of minutes. Sometimes the commercial mail drop companies are even better because then you can have an actual street address, and your actual "box" will be notated as a "suite." A great shield to utilize, especially if you need to get a new driver's license, personal or business checks, etc.

Why?

Because debt collectors are very creative and resourceful types who have ways—many ways—to track you down. So are process servers. Throw up some obstacles. Make them see you on your terms, or make them work awfully damned hard to find you.

By the way, I don't want to hear any excuses. I know money is tight right now, but what price can you place on your sanity? Do it. It'll do wonders for your state of mind.

Incidentally: If you're required to give them a street address of your actual home, consider giving them the address of your attorney. You don't have an attorney? Give them the address of your best friend or a family member you can depend on. Enough said.

STEP TWO: Go to your nearest post office and get a handful of "change of address" forms and fill them out. Get the post office to begin forwarding all of your mail to your new address at once. Notify your creditors of your new address and breathe a little easier. You've started creating some distance.

"I'M SORRY. THE NUMBER YOU HAVE DIALED IS NO LONGER IN SERVICE . . . ."

Ahhhh, yes. *The telephone.* The greatest invention ever created in the eyes of the debt collectors across the country. The tool of location. The tool of interrogation. The tool of intimidation. The tool of tele-terrorists.

Why some people continue to answer their phone when they're heading towards difficult financial times never ceases to amaze me. This inanimate device that allows the debt collector into your home at any hour of the day or night is so easy to control.

STEP ONE: Change the number. I know it's obvious, but sometimes those are the things that elude all of us. Change the number immediately. Call the phone company and tell them you've been receiving obscene or harassing phone calls and you need the number changed at once.

STEP TWO: Before you hang up on your protectors of privacy at the phone company, tell them that you need the new number to be UN-listed and NON-published. Instruct them that you want your address to be UN-listed and NON-published as well.

STEP THREE: At the same time, be sure to give them your new mailing address.

STEP FOUR: Request a "password" on your account. Anyone calling in to the phone company posing as you or your spouse had better know the password or they'll be shut out of any information. Use a word or name that you will be able to easily remember (or if you're like me, write it down somewhere where you won't lose it), but don't use your spouse's name or middle name, your or your spouse's mother's name, etc. because those creative debt collectors can find out just about anything from your credit files. And they know how to use it.

BONUS SAFETY TIP #1: If you have a friend or relative with a different last name that trusts you and is willing to help you out, consider this: Disconnect your old phone number and turn off your account altogether. Have your friend or relative open a new telephone account in their name at your current physical address. The upside to this technique? Once again I remind you of the creative and devious mind of the debt collector. They have been known to "pop" an unlisted number through friends/contacts in the telephone business. This way they can't—your name is never listed for the number. The downside? You may have a hard time convincing your friend or relative to take on the potential liability of a telephone bill in the event you default. After all, you're up to your rear in alligators right now. What assurances do they have that you won't stick them with a huge phone bill? I don't blame them, and neither should you.

BONUS SAFETY TIP #2: Get a voicemail phone number. They're easy to find and as cheap as $5-7 a month. Many of the voicemail systems will page you if you have a pager, making it easier for you to pick up your calls as they come in. By having this number you can give out a contact number for people to call you, including your family and friends. Don't forget: the debt collectors will call those people on your credit applications first, usually your family and friends, and weasel your new phone number out of them. Some are successful because they're great liars . . . others are assisted by friends or family members that are either not clued in to what's going on or are, shall we say, "mentally challenged" in the area of common sense. Don't give those people a chance to break through your safety shield. Give them the voicemail number.

BONUS SAFETY TIP #3: If you should return a phone call to a creditor or debt collector, saving money and calling them back on their toll-free "800 number," _**beware!**_ Any company that has an "800 number" and is in the business of collecting debts may frequently utilize a little-known fact about these numbers. Every time you call in to a toll-free number the phone company providing the service can provide their subscriber with an "ANI" listing. "ANI" stands for "Automatic Number Identifier," a technical way of saying that every time you call in on an "800 number" the party on the receiving end instantly (in many cases) knows the telephone number from which you're calling. American Express used to use this service extensively, in the name of high-tech customer service. An American Express cardholder would call in from their home and the operator who answered would say: "Good evening, Mr. Dover! What can we do for you this evening?" At first everyone thought this would be really cool and show that American Express was really the trendsetter . . . really on top of things. But then the negative backlash came. Big Brother was watching! And how! Not only would the operator at American Express know who was calling, but they'd have all of your account information in front of them on their screen. (Apparently this didn't go over well with American Express customers . . . AMEX service representatives don't do this anymore.)

Pretty intimidating stuff.

Don't think your friendly debt collector would ever hesitate in using the same technology to find your new "unlisted" phone number. Be smart if you want to save money and communicate with your creditors. Use a pay phone. Hotel lobbies always have quiet areas where you can make your calls safely.

YOUR LICENSE TO PRIVACY . . . _NOT!_

I really get irritated with states around the country that are using your Social Security Number as your driver's license number. This is gross intrusion, an enormous invasion of your privacy. Driver's license information in many states is very easy to obtain, although some states have begun restricting public disclosure of this information. (Unfortunately, it took the murder of actress Rebecca Schaeffer several years ago at the hands of a deranged fan who got her address from public driver's license records to finally change this outdated practice.) Nevertheless, it's still easy to obtain this information if you know where to go. So this is obviously another potential breach in your newfound shield of privacy. Next stop: The Department of Motor Vehicles or whatever agency is empowered with driver's license and automobile registration and/or issuance.

STEP ONE: Change your address on your driver's license. Many states require a street address; this is where your mail-drop service address comes in handy and works much better than a U.S. Post Office mailbox. Do it at once!

STEP TWO: Change the address on your motor vehicle registration. You know how easy it is to run a license plate by now, don't you? Get with the program here! Head off your opposition at the pass and keep your armor or privacy intact.

YOUR BANK ACCOUNT...
THE LAST STOP ON THE INSULATION EXPRESS

Now that you've gotten your address, your phone number, your driver's license and vehicle registration all changed to your new address, finish up at your bank.

STEP ONE: If you still have a checking account, immediately change the address on your checks and account information. The fewer questions the better: Notify the bank in writing, through the mail, of your new address. Be sure to include a photocopy of one of your deposit slips, along with a copy of your new driver's license (you know, the one showing your new address, right?). Give the bank the new mailing address information and if you obtained a voicemail, give them that number as your new phone number. Don't think that a bank will keep all of your information private. Sometimes people make mistakes . . . and people work at banks. Be smart, not sorry.

STEP TWO: When you re-order your checks, be sure to include only your name and mailing address. *NOTHING ELSE!*

I'm amazed by the life histories some people put on the front of their checks. Full names, street addresses, home telephone numbers, his driver's license number, her driver's license number, his Social Security Number, her Social Security Number. Why don't you just attach a copy of your last three years' income tax returns while you're at it? Wake up, America! Think about how many people handle one of your checks. How many clerks in the stores look at the front of your checks. They know everything they need to find out anything they want about you, including not just your financial information, but medical information as well.

Big Brother is alive and well in the 1990s, thank you.

THERE'S A STORMFRONT COMING

Do you or your spouse have any judgments coming your way in the near future? Any liens, garnishments or even lawsuits getting ready to take root? Then you'd better read on . . . .

This country is comprised of 50 states with 50 potentially very different sets of laws governing debtor's rights. States like Texas and Florida are very kind to debtors and protective of their assets. Most are not. This is where good advice, insight and knowledge prove their worth.

I highly recommend these two terrific books (and I didn't write either one!): **PERSONAL BANKRUPTCY and Debt Adjustment**, by Kenneth J. Doran, is published by Random House and sells for around $10. I'm not telling you to file or even think about filing for bankruptcy, but this book has a list in its appendix of the personal property exemptions, state by state. It tells you what's exempt from creditors and what's not, and I think it's a good start for those trying to become bulletproof.

The second book is **ASSET PROTECTION SECRETS**, by Arnold S. Goldstein. It's published by Garrett Publishing of Deerfield Beach, Florida. I've had Arnie on my radio show and I can tell you without any hesitation, he knows his stuff. From asset protection planning to making yourself 100% creditor-proof to analyzing laws that automatically shield many assets, this is a must read. At times it's a little technical, but that's the nature of the beast. Besides, he's an attorney. Enough said.

By using foresight in estate planning and techniques encompassing the use of children's or family trusts that are perfectly legal and legitimate, you stand a much better chance of weathering the storm. Otherwise you're like the guy standing flat-footed in the center of the train tracks, looking for the light at the end of the tunnel.

Unfortunately, that light at the end of the tunnel is a train.

Wise up or lose it all. Legally plan and protect whatever assets you may have left or risk losing everything.

The choice is yours.

10

4½ STEPS TO ELIMINATING THE DEBT COLLECTOR

"Nothing is more terrible than activity without insight."
Thomas Carlyle

You'll hear me continue to repeat this throughout this book:

KNOWLEDGE IS *POWER*

Before you get involved in a battle, you'd better know exactly who your opponent is.

This is absolutely the <u>MOST IMPORTANT</u> chapter of this book. This is your blueprint for eliminating your friendly debt collector. I suggest you read this chapter at **least** two or three times.

If you are contacted by a debt collector—

❑**STEP ONE:** Figure out *who* you're dealing with. Directly ask the person calling you at work or at home the following questions:

1) What is your name?
2) What is your title?
3) What is your phone number?
4) May I have the name of your company?
5) May I have your mailing address?

Be very courteous. There's no need to be combative.

Just tell them that you are working at trying to get out of the mess you're in financially and really want to get this debt paid off, but you need to keep everything straight and need this information.

Don't let them upset you.

Don't let them start quizzing you.

Don't be sucked into their game by answering their questions before they've told youthe answers to the five questions I just gave you.

Stand firm and tell them you want to get this whole mess behind you, but you are keeping good records on who you are paying back and how much. *"And if you want to collect any money on this debt, I need to get this information first . . ."*

After all (you'll tell them), *"You're just a voice on the telephone. I want to send you the money I owe, but I need to know who I'm working with . . . don't you think?"*

These are money-motivated people. They smell a quick commission. An easy mark. Someone who is asking a few questions, but sounds reasonable. Ahhhh, yes. A quick payday.

"Would you do me a favor?" you ask the tele-terrorist. *"Would you send me a letter with all of the information I just asked for, plus the information about my overdue account? I'd really feel much better about sending you this money if I had something in writing not only confirming the amounts owed and where I need to send you my . . . would you like a check or a money order?"*

The debt collector will be doing everything in their

power to keep the excitement out of their voice. They may also attempt to press you for money now. Remember, don't agree to anything. If you need your memory refreshed, go back and re-read Chapter 4.

Hold your ground. Get this very important information from them . . . up front.

❏**STEP ONE-AND-A-HALF:** If the debt collector won't play ball and send you a letter, then get all of this information over the phone. Don't delay. Go directly to the next step . . . and *enjoy!*

❏**STEP TWO:** As soon as you get this information in the mail from them, fire out the Cease & Desist letter— always via certified mail. A sample is located in Appendix C, along with instructions on how to send certified mail covered in Appendix D.

Write that letter and get it out in the mail immediately. Don't even think about cutting corners. Send the letter via Certified Mail/Return Receipt Requested, or don't waste your time sending the letter at all.

You must send the letter via Certified Mail/Return Receipt Requested in order to effectively invoke federal law! Don't ask questions. Just do it. Then . . .

Turn on your favorite music.

Pour yourself your favorite drink.

Savor the moment.

❏**STEP THREE:** If you really want to be prepared and keep great notes for future use (just in case), go to the local office supply and buy yourself a large day-by-day appointment book. Make sure this book has plenty of lines to write notes about the day's events, hour-by-hour.

Why do you need this?

You need this to keep all of your notes straight. Confusion is the last thing you need right now, and if you document your attack plan at every turn, you've got 98% of the battle won!

a) Keep this daily planner by the phone you use the most. You know the one. The phone that you make the majority of your phone calls from, the one you usually answer.

b) If the debt collector calls and you don't have your book near by, ask them to either call back or put the phone down and go get your book. Make them wait. After all, they're invading your privacy.

c) If you have call waiting, have the phone company remove it. First off, it's an added expense you can do without right now. Secondly and most importantly, if you're involved in another telephone conversation with a prospective employer, an ex-spouse or maybe even another debt collector, chances are your emotions could be running high. These emotions will set you up and make you vulnerable and susceptible to mistakes. Don't worry. If the phone is busy, the debt collector will call back.

d) Make a note of your first contact with the debt collector. Write down as much information as possible, making sure to note the time of day they called.

e) Be sure to notate all additional calls from the debt

collector. Specify the time they called and the name of the person calling and what account they're attempting to collect. This is important. Write down as much of the conversation as you can.

f) Be sure to note in this same book the day/date you mailed your Cease & Desist letter to the debt collector. Note the account information and the collection agency/name of the individual collector you mailed to. Note the Certified Mail Receipt Number.

g) When you receive the green card/receipt back from the post office, make a note of the date the debt collector received your letter. Note the name of the person that signed for the letter (if you can figure it out).

h) <u>VERY IMPORTANT!</u> Make a note of the next contact made by the debt collector after they received your letter. Circle it in red! This is very important, since under federal law the debt collector can only contact you one more time after they have received notice that you are not dealing with them. (Remember that Cease & Desist letter you hammered them with?) Every call they make or letter they send you after their ONE LAST CONTACT (as allowed under federal law) after receiving your Cease & Desist Letter via Certified Mail/Return Receipt mail is a violation of Public Law 95-109, the Fair Debt Collections Practices Act. The better you document every phone call and every letter, the better chances are of burying the debt collector. Wouldn't that be nice? It's fun to turn the tables on the debt collectors!

i) You may want to go by your local Radio Shack and

get a telephone recording device. You plug this little gem into a cassette tape recorder and your telephone. They sell for under $20 and will give you even more confidence when you know that your telephone conversations are being taped. Not only will this give you a record of what was said, but it will provide you with some terrific leverage if the debt collector is true to form and crosses the line and begins breaking laws by lying, misrepresenting or using foul language. You may have to restrain the glee in your voice because their phone calls will soon become the highlight of your day. What's that old saying? *Turnabout is fair play.*

FIND OUT WHAT THEY'RE SAYING ABOUT YOU

You have **got** to know what's being reported about your credit history as you work your way through the debt collection nightmare. The way these accounts are going to be reported is a crucial part of your negotiations . . . with the original creditor.

❑**STEP FOUR:** **Know what your creditors and their hired-gun debt collectors are saying about you!**

You must first start this game with all of the cards in the deck. You must know what has been reported about your outstanding debts. This means you'll be contacting all three of the national credit bureaus and get copies of all three of your credit bureau reports.

I realize that there may be local or regional credit

reporting bureaus/agencies in your area, but these companies generally rely on the information collected by one of the "Big Three"—TRW, CSC/Equifax, and TransUnion.

As a result of a settlement of a class action lawsuit initiated by the Texas State Attorney General's Office a few years ago, TRW agreed to give Americans one free* copy of their credit bureau report annually . . . just for asking!

What a deal! So send away for your **free** TRW report immediately, before proceeding any further with any attempts to evaluate your current credit profile and how it relates to your quest to settle all of your debts with the original creditors.

While we're on the subject of TRW, you must be sure to include with your letter requesting a free copy of your credit bureau report some form of "positive identification." Their position is that it's to "ensure privacy," so give them what they need, but **ONLY** what they need.

Here's what I mean. TRW will ask for:

"*. . . a copy of a proof of address document containing your name and current address*"

or

"*. . . a current billing statement from a major creditor, a utility bill such as cable TV, gas, electric, water or*

---

* If you have been turned down for credit within the last sixty (60) days, under the Fair Credit Reporting Act (which we'll discuss in greater detail later in this book) you are entitled to a free copy of your report, even if you've already received your annual free one from TRW. That's the law, but it only applies if you have been turned down for credit recently, and if the potential credit grantor used TRW as their source of information on which to base their opinion. Any "turndown" letter you may have received from potential credit grantors will state the source of information upon which they based their denial towards the bottom of the letter. This source must provide you with a free report if you request this report within sixty (60) days of the turndown.

telephone; or a valid driver's license issued with your current address."

Okay. So they're trying to protect your privacy, huh? Then give them only what they need: a cover letter from you with all of the appropriate information and a document showing your name and current mail/home/billing address. **But nothing else.**

That means that if you send them a copy of the first page of your telephone bill, use a black marker and black out the <u>entire</u> telephone number or any other account number; if you send them a copy of a utility bill, black out <u>all</u> account numbers (including those that may be encoded in a long, multi-numbered sequence across the very top or very bottom of the bill). Same thing goes for any credit card account statements. And be sure to black out any account balance information, including balance owed and payment currently due. It's <u>none</u> of their business. Give them only what they requested.

Nothing more. In short, you need to show TRW that you have a valid account, but you do not need to reveal information <u>about</u> the account.

If you decide to send them a copy of your current driver's license, be sure to black out the line of information containing your driver's license number. You may also choose to black out height, weight, eye color, hair color and other restrictions/information on your license. Finally, you may wish to black out your picture while you're at it. Remember, they wanted proof of identification with your current home/mailing address on it, so give it to them.

But nothing else. It's none of their business, so why give them all of this additional information that they could potentially use, re-sell or put into their own computer data banks? It's none of their business. Don't forget this!

TRW

Here's the current address/phone number for TRW. This could change and if it does, ask your local directory assistance operator or 800 directory assistance (800) 555-1212) operator for the local/regional TRW office that you need to consult.

TRW Complimentary Credit Report
P.O. Box 2350
Chatsworth, CA 91313-2350
(800) 862-7654

Remember, TRW can change their mailing address at any time so be sure to call their TOLL FREE number listed above FIRST to make sure this address we are providing is correct.

If you wish to write to lodge a complaint or start your journey up the chain of command, try this address or phone number (phone numbers are always subject to change):

TRW
ATTN: NCAC
P.O. Box 2104
Allen, TX 75002

Please use the CREDIT BUREAU REPORT REQUEST LETTER form located in Appendix B at the back of this book to get your report, and follow the letter format provided.

CSC/Equifax

CSC/Equifax also services various parts of the country, so the correct address to request a copy of your current credit bureau report could be different from region to region.

CSC/Equifax isn't as charitable as our good friends at TRW so this report will cost you. But it's money well spent; you've got to know what everyone is saying about you (and your spouse if you're married) before you attack your current situation.

Here are two **TOLL-FREE** numbers for you to call CSC/Equifax:

(800) 759-5979 or (800) 685-1111

If you want to write to them, try this address:

**CSC/Equifax
Post Office Box 740241
Atlanta, GA 30375**

Again, CSC/Equifax will ask you for the usual data, including a copy of your current driver's license, but be sure to black out data that does not pertain to this process (like height, weight, eye color, hair color and other restrictions information).

CSC/Equifax will charge you for this report: An average fee of $3 (thanks to recent changes in the Fair Credit Reporting Act and Congressman Joseph P. Kennedy [D-Massachusetts]) is the prevailing rate, but call the 800 number first and get all of the specifics before you sit down to write your letter. (Remember, *BACK OFF!* makes it really easy for you to get this report; to make this part of the process a no-brainer, use a copy of the CREDIT BUREAU REPORT REQUEST LETTER form in Appendix B, page 157.)

By the way, when you send the money to CSC/Equifax for your copy of your report, I strongly URGE you to send them a money order, readily available at the post office or convenience stores across the country.

Why?

When you send them a personal check, you're allowing a few things to occur:

a) They may sit on your report for an extra 10-14 days waiting for your "check to clear" their bank;

b) You're giving them all the information that is printed across the front of your check;

c) You're giving them the name, location/branch and account number of your checking account.

Am I sounding paranoid?

Perhaps.

But don't ever lose sight of the type of the business TRW, Equifax and Trans Union are all in: the collection, sale and re-sale of information on **YOU**.

The front of your check tells a story. It's up to you whether you wish to tell them **your** story . . . or not.

TRANSUNION

They're the easiest and quickest to deal with if you've been turned down for credit recently. No 800 number here, but a voicemail-type, touchtone prompting system that gets your report out to you quickly.

Again, if you have been denied credit within the last thirty days, federal laws dictate that they provide you a "freebie" report upon request. Contact them at their main consumer assistance number:

(800) 851-2674

An automated, prompting telephone attendant line may be quicker, though it'll cost you since it's not toll free. But it's faster:
(313) 689-3888

Their main office address if you wish to write is:

TransUnion
P.O. Box 7000
North Olmstead, OH 44070

Trans Union also has three regional offices if you wish to contact these in your part of the country:

P.O. Box 360
Philadelphia, PA 19105
(215) 569-4582

South First St., Suite 201
Louisville, KY 40202
(502) 584-0121

P.O. Box 3110
Fullerton, CA 92634
(714) 738-3800

The computer will prompt you and ask the basic questions: first name, last name, address, city, state, zip code, social security number, date of birth and finally, whether you've moved in the last 2 years (or not). They promise to send your report out within 72 hours.

However, if you wish to simply obtain a copy of your report for your own personal information you'll need to send them the appropriate fee accompanied by all of the appropriate information as outlined above, with one addition—they also want to know the name of your current employer and their telephone number.

As far as I'm concerned, **it's none of their business**. It is <u>not</u> relevant to your request for your information from their files.

<u>Refuse</u> to give it to them! Follow my form letter outlined in Appendix B at the back of the book, send them the appropriate amount of money <u>in money order form</u> and see what happens.

Your first steps toward regaining control of your life begin with obtaining copies of all three of the national credit bureau reports:

TRW
CSC/Equifax
Trans Union

Get those reports in your hands and move ahead to your next challenge, but keep these facts in mind:

• There are over 1,100 credit and mortgage reporting companies in the United States

• There are more than 450 million credit files on American consumers

• 1 in 2 people who view their credit reports end up disputing information

• 75% of those disputes were corrected by the credit reporting agency

• One of the favorite techniques of the debt collector is blackmailing you with negative information on your credit report

If you don't know what your files say about you, you are being both blind and foolish. The chances are 1 in 2 that your files contain erroneous information. The chances of you already having negative information on your credit report if you've been dealing with one or more debt collectors for any length of time is a frightening 95 out of 100. Start smart- deal from strength. Knowledge is power!

And remember . . . your only leverage when you begin repaying your past due/renegotiated debts is the cash you have in your hand. If you don't get the creditors to agree to delete any negative information about your account before you've repaid the debt, you're screwed. You've given up your only hammer. Be honest. Be ethical. But be smart . . . and *play to win!*

SAME ACCOUNT . . .
NEW DEBT COLLECTION AGENCY

Once you've hammered your friends at the debt collection agency with your Cease & Desist letter (they call it "being Cease-Commed") expect one of the following actions:

1) The debt collector will turn your account over to the original creditor;

2) The debt collector will turn the account over to an attorney to sue you;

3) The original creditor, after having your account given up by the collection agency as a result of your Cease & Desist letter, will assign your account to another collection agency;

4) The original creditor will assign it to an attorney to sue you;

5) The original creditor will realize they're not going to get anything from you easily, will simply "write off" your account as uncollectible, and you won't hear anything again.

Let's look at these one by one.

1) DEBT COLLECTOR TURNS YOUR ACCOUNT OVER TO THE ORIGINAL CREDITOR. No need for you to take any action here; we're back at square one. Wait and see what the original creditor does.

2) DEBT COLLECTOR GETS AN ATTORNEY TO SUE YOU. If you had the money in the first place you would have paid them, right? If the attorney contacts you, send the attorney a Cease & Desist letter. Remember, some attorneys makes lots of money threatening consumers with lawsuits and collecting debts. If an attorney collects 2 or more debts a year, they're debt collectors. Take them out with the Cease & Desist letter. If they sue you, they sue you. You don't have the money anyway, so it doesn't mean they're going to collect anything!

3) ORIGINAL CREDITOR GETS THE ACCOUNT BACK AND ASSIGNS IT TO ANOTHER COLLECTOR. So they assign it to another collection agency. You know what to do, right? Send them a Cease & Desist letter. Believe me, it will work again. If they want to send it to another collector, that's their decision. It's your right not to deal with the debt collector.

4) ORIGINAL CREDITOR HIRES AN ATTORNEY TO SUE YOU. See #2 above; follow the same course of action.

5) ORIGINAL CREDITOR DOES NOTHING AND WRITES YOUR DEBT OFF. Now you're in a position of negotiation that will allow you to repay the debt. If you can repay the debt under revised terms, then do it! If you can pay back 100 cents on every dollar you owe them, terrific! But remember, by their assigning your account to a debt collector they as much as told you that they're willing to take less. The debt collectors don't work for free . . . the original creditor was willing to give the debt collector 30- 50% of what they collected. Why won't the original creditor let you settle for 50-70% of what you owe them? They almost always will! But you've got to be aggressive, deal with the right person in the company (not some toll-free service representative with little influence) and get it in writing.

And make *damned* sure that they agree to delete **all** information about this account, placed either by them or any collection agencies or attorneys that attempted to collect the account, from all credit reporting bureaus in the nation. Period. End of discussion. If they don't agree, I guess they don't want their money.

IN SUMMARY: This is an extremely important chapter . . . one that I suggest you read and reread several times. Debt collectors are predictable; the insights you have gained from this chapter will help you avoid making costly mistakes. The more familiar you are with this material, the better off you will be.

11

CREATE
WORKOUTS

You can't get blood out of a turnip. Or a rock.

I mean it. No matter how hard you press, no matter how hard you try, it *still* can't be done. It's sort of like being out of cash. What's the creditor going to do? You try to explain your situation, but "they" have their rules and that's that. *"If you can't pay, we'll just have to refer your account to our collection agency . . ."* Whoa, now you're scared. Yeah, *right*.

We've already solved the debt collector problem. You're not going to pay them. You know how to take them out by now. And when you do, your account gets kicked back to the original creditor. I know they might throw it back to another debt collection agency, but you'll get rid of them easy enough. You'll wear them down. You have the knowledge. You have the insight.

And don't forget: You have the upper hand. *You have the money. Maybe not right now, but eventually, you will have the money to pay the original creditor.*

Since I already know that you are going to order copies of all three of your credit bureau reports (and your spouse's if you're married), this will be your first

step towards gaining the insight necessary to renegotiate, and hopefully repay, your debts.

You know that you had better not agree to paying out
a restructured debt unless you are 99.9% sure that you'll
be able to live up to those revised terms. Otherwise,
you've probably shot yourself in the foot for the last
time with the creditor. They've heard it all before, and
even though your intentions were noble enough and you
really were going to repay them (honest!) it doesn't
matter anymore. They'd rather take the loss and move
on. If we're talking about a large enough sum of money
you owe to the creditor, they may spend the effort to sue
you.

How does the creditor evaluate you? What do they
base their "to sue or not to sue, that is the question"
upon?

In most cases, your credit bureau reports.

All of those accounts being charged off . . . all of
those R9 and I9 notations . . . all of those debt collector
activity notations can be your best front-line defense
against your creditors. After all, your creditors have
already lost whatever amount of money you owe them.
Why should they throw good money after bad? It
doesn't make sense to pursue a judgment if they'll never
collect it. And once they get a look at all of your problems on your credit bureau report, they'll know they
have only two chances to collect any money from you:
SLIM and NONE.

You see, sometimes the credit bureaus can be helpful!

YOU'RE 60 DAYS BEHIND
ON YOUR CAR PAYMENT

Remember back in Chapter 6 when I discussed "secured" versus "unsecured" creditors? This is a classic example of a secured lender that will always get its security back, so be smart and soften the impact.

If you know you're heading for some bumpy financial roads ahead and are going to get behind on your car payment, consider following these steps:

1) If you have enough equity in your car, try to sell it and get some cash out of it instead of giving it up through repossession;

2) Begin working on buying a decent and (hopefully) reliable new or used car before you destroy your credit;

3) Apply the monies you would have made on your current car to the replacement car down payment until you have enough money to purchase a replacement car;

4) As soon as you have gotten your replacement car, contact the company that has financed/leased the car you can't afford and tell them you wish to turn the car over to them. Get all of your personal possessions out of the car . . . and don't trash it. Clean it up and handle this "voluntary repossession" with class and dignity. Doing this may come in handy later.

5) Try to work out a deal with the finance/lease company on how the repossession will show up on your credit report. They may be willing to work out a settlement on the balance owed on the car (after they sell it; this is known as a "deficiency balance") if you pay this

amount (once you've gotten your financial situation back under control). All you can do is try. The worst they can do is say no. Many finance companies won't waste any time trying to come after you for the deficit owed. It's not worth the headache.

Remember, if you turn the car over on a voluntary repossession, the amount you owe later on will be less because the finance/lease company won't have to employ a "repo man" to find and repossess your car. These guys get anywhere from $200-500 to locate and re-acquire automobiles, so it makes sense that if they don't have to find your car and tow it away, that's one less expense you'll end up owing them. Don't play "cat and mouse." They'll always find the car, and probably at the most inopportune time.

YOUR MONTHLY HOUSEPAYMENT . . . YOUR MONTHLY ADVENTURE

Once again, this is another example of a secured creditor that will always be in a position to repossess its security. Foreclosing on a house can be a real nightmare, but as I said back in Chapter 4, you can turn a negative situation into one that is tolerable to both parties. Go back and review the strategies outlined in Chapter 6 and get your housing situation under control.

UNSECURED CREDITORS . . . THE CLOCK IS TICKING

Since unsecured creditors can do little more than feed you to the debt collectors or threaten you with a lawsuit, there's not a whole lot to worry about. You already know how to take the debt collectors out of the picture. You already know not to commit to repaying any creditors unless you're absolutely sure you can deliver. You already know that there are no debtors prisons, and that if your creditor report is torn up this usually reduces the chances of any creditor, especially an unsecured one, pursuing a lawsuit against you.

Call your local free legal clinic, or perhaps a local college or university that has a school of law. Maybe a friend is an attorney, or has one they can call upon to get an important question answered. Here's what you need to determine for the state in which you are currently residing: *"What is the statute of limitations on the enforcement/collectibility of an unsecured debt?"*

This is an important number.

This timeframe and concept apply to creditors like VISA, MasterCard, American Express, Discover, Mobil, Shell, Sears . . . you get the idea. Revolving credit line-type unsecured debts. Installment contracts get complicated, and I'm not about to try to practice law. That's what lawyers are for. But the majority of your unsecured credit cards, plus medical debts owed to doctors, laboratories, hospitals, etc., usually fall into this category.

Your leverage goes up dramatically once the collectibility of a debt has passed. Once you've passed through the window of time that a creditor can sue you for defaulting on your debt, your leverage goes through the roof. Many companies will still encourage debt collectors to attempt to collect on these debts, but once you've made it clear to the debt collector that they're history (you know the old Cease & Desist letter routine) and made it equally clear to the creditor that you know the law and their debt is no longer collectible, then it's time to get this mess cleaned up and behind you, once and for all. Once the original creditor knows that you know what the statute of limitations is on that debt they will become much more willing to get something. Or they may become enraged and just sit tight and be satisfied with screwing up your credit report for the maximum period of time possible. The smart companies will work to recover whatever monies they can, so go make a deal. Use the Original Creditor/Old Debt Settlement letter format in Appendix E to handle this.

NOTE: This timeframe averages 4 years across the nation, but some states are known to allow debts to be enforceable for up to 6 years, so be sure to check on this before you get drunk with a little knowledge. This could blow up in your face if you make some incorrect assumptions.

A WARNING TO FEDERAL WORKERS

I love the way the laws of our country are passed.

Totally unrelated proposed laws end up attached to pieces of legislation in the eleventh hour in the name of getting votes, and this type of wrangling has now put federal workers at risk.

As of February 3, 1994 federal workers are now vulnerable to debt collection just like the private sector. Up until this law was tagged onto an updated Hatch "No Politics" Act, the only federal workers at risk were postal employees. Now all federal agencies will allow garnishment through payroll deductions just like the rest of us . . . all the more reason to know the right "buttons" to push and the right moves to make during your negotiations. Sometimes, most of the time, your best weapon is your willingness to bluff.

THE THREAT OF BANKRUPTCY

Negotiating settlements for unsecured debts before the collectibility/enforcement runs out takes a little more finesse, and a lot more guts. If you like to play poker, you may enjoy this phase of the recovery.

If you tell your unsecured creditors up front and early on that you cannot pay them but want to, that you just need some time and breathing room, you'll be lucky if 2 out of 10 agree to work with you.

"I'm sorry, this is the minimum amount we can accept!"

"We can give you a reduced payment plan for 6 months, then it's back to your normally scheduled payment plan."

"We can't allow you to not make payments for a year!"

Most of these creditors, showing their infinite wisdom and foresight, will simply assign your account to some outside/third party debt collector that you'll make short order of with your Cease & Desist letters. Then, when your account is kicked back to the original creditor, maybe they'll be ready to negotiate. And maybe not.

The chances are good that you'll have to go through the debt collector cycle at least one or two times before the original creditor finally "gets" it. Everyone would be saved so much brain damage if the big creditors across the country would wake up. Maybe this book will force them to start working with consumers on a friendly basis instead of going through all of these inane debt collector gyrations. Or worse yet for everyone involved, ending up in bankruptcy court.

The unsecured/credit card creditors know that if a consumer decides to take a bankruptcy, they'll probably end up with nothing.

By the time your debt has gone through a cycle or two of debt collector and reassignment to the original creditor, your credit report is wasted and you're tired and maybe even broke. The original creditor has charged off your account as a "Bad Debt Expense," so any money they collect from you goes straight to their bottom line. It's pure profit now, a bonus they didn't expect. So it's up to you to shake them hard enough and wake them up and convince them to deal.

Use the letter in Appendix F and make your position crystal clear: If they wish to pursue you and take you to court in hopes of getting a judgment, fine. That's their prerogative. But you're giving them fair warning that if they do get their judgment you'll dispose of them and the other creditors in bankruptcy court. Quick, clean and protected by federal law.

This is your bluff, of course. You already know how I feel about bankruptcy court. But keep in mind that they can always sue you because that's their right. You need to determine by the tone of their correspondence (since your telephone number was changed and unlisted a long time ago, right?) if they do intend to sue you. If it is referred to an attorney I can just about guarantee the attorney's unwillingness to deal, since they get paid regardless. But if you don't have the money in the first place, we're back again where we started, and everybody loses.

You can't get blood out of a turnip, can you?

Just because they get a judgment doesn't mean they'll be able to collect it.

Please don't forget an earlier lesson that I will remind you of one more time:

An attorney who collects two or more debts in a year is considered a debt collector. Don't get scared just because you're being threatened by a debt collector. Send the attorney a Cease & Desist letter and see what happens. If they're serious about suing you, you'll find out pretty quickly.

Even if they do get a judgment, you may frequently buy the judgment back for a fraction of its value through an "unrelated third party." Get advice from a qualified attorney before trying this ploy. This particular technique was used with great frequency by many of my friends digging out of their respective messes in Texas in the late 1980s. I saw them do it. I've seen others in other states around the country do it. It's a game of nerves and not suggested for the faint of heart, but a game that can be played and won more times than it's lost.

Go back and re-read Chapter 4 and review the debt collector's schedule of expected recoveries for past due accounts. By now you should already have a different feel for this whole game, far more different than you did the first time you read the chapter. It's like a puzzle . . . all of the pieces are now falling into place.

Don't get your feelings hurt by taking things personally. Remember, all a creditor can do when you make a pass at settling for an amount less than face value is say "no."

You tried . . . you failed.

So what?

They don't get paid, and it was their choice. Would you rather have something or nothing? If the roles were reversed, what would you do? That's why you have more power in a situation like this than you think—so use it.

12

FINAL THOUGHTS BEFORE YOU GO TO WAR

*"To sin by silence when we should protest
makes cowards out of men."*
Ella Wheeler Wilcox

Don't **ever** allow these tele-terrorists to bully you. The only way debt collectors that routinely break federal laws in the name of getting you to pay your bills are going to be stopped is by people like you putting your foot down.

There's nothing to be ashamed of; everyone has either experienced money problems themselves or known someone close to them who has. Whatever your situation may be, it's not going to shock your state Attorney General's office. It's not going to unnerve your regional Federal Trade Commission officials. They've seen it all and heard it all before.

They also know that consumers forced to endure these unscrupulous tactics at the hands of debt collectors are ashamed to admit to anyone, especially a stranger, that they're having financial difficulties . . . and this pride keeps them from notifying the proper authorities.

Please—don't let this happen to you!

If someone is breaking federal law while collecting a

debt, they must be stopped. Any report you file with the Federal Trade Commission or the Attorney General is confidential. Nobody will be able to get their hands on these files and read about your personal situation. Nobody will be able to get an insight into your private life. I know this because I tried to obtain files under the Freedom of Information Act and was turned down because it would have violated the consumers' right to privacy. I understood and accepted it. I only wanted to research the violations that had been reported to the authorities.

If consumers across America fail to speak up and voice their displeasure with the system, we are all sentenced to suffer in a segment of society that's not only broken, but being looted by a bunch of punks that hide behind the telephones and doors of the debt collection industry.

You've got no excuse for not writing if your rights as a consumer are being violated! Appendix J offers a list of all of the regional Federal Trade Commission offices. For your convenience, Appendix I furnishes a sample complaint letter to the FTC. Use the same letter format to complain to your state's attorney general.

Please use it.

More importantly, follow up when you receive the FTC's standard complaint form. Follow up, document your complaint and push them to the point of resolution. If you don't make your voice heard, you've just wasted $15 on this book. Or maybe not . . . give it to a friend or relative.

YOU WILL SURVIVE

By the time you've climbed out of the pit of uncertainty, anxiety and fear that your world has become, you'll feel smarter. You'll feel stronger. You'll have learned so much about yourself and your ability to just survive.

You may grow impatient with others that haven't yet "been there" when they complain about how tough their lives are. You'll probably have newfound compassion for those who are experiencing tough times . . . for those who are being forced to endure difficult days and long, sleepless nights.

And you'll probably have acquired a keen distaste for the debt collection industry and their predictably sleazy tactics.

Perhaps you'll have developed a new level of disdain for creditors who would rather shoot themselves in the foot and "prove to you who's in charge" by failing to negotiate with you and work things out . . . instead choosing to sue you and obtain a judgment.

You **will** survive this phase of your life and emerge much smarter with (hopefully) a higher degree of respect for credit cards and a desire to live a more "debt-free" lifestyle.

This book will probably look like it's been through a war, too.

You will find yourself going back and referring to this book time and time again. You'll be amazed when you read this book and hear some of the very same lines you're hearing or reading right now. You'll really be impressed when some of the events that I predict actually come true, just as I said they would. You'll ask yourself: "How did he know that?" and your confidence will grow as you utilize the techniques and ideas I have shared with you throughout this book.

I know this stuff because I've been there.

I survived.

My only regret is that I wish I knew then what I know now. I learned it all the hard way. But look at all of the pain and suffering you are about to avoid! You will benefit from my past experiences . . . and recover from your own personal hell faster than I did. I promise.

Money just isn't worth losing sleep over.

It's not worth fighting with your spouse over.

It's not worth losing your temper and screaming at the kids over.

It's not worth breaking up a family over.

It's not worth taking stupid chances over.

It's not worth breaking the law over.

They say that "desperate men do desperate things," and I understand this, too. But the almighty dollar just isn't worth it.

Get creative!

Slash your spending. Use coupons. Work extra jobs. Do whatever it takes to make ends meet. But most importantly, arm yourself with the knowledge I've compiled in this book and get ready to go to war. Your goal is to emerge with your dignity intact and reduce your time in the "credit penalty box" courtesy of TRW, CSC/Equifax and TransUnion.

Debt collectors lie and mislead and say whatever it takes to get you to send them money. Who are you going to believe, them or me? I'm not the one shaking you down over the telephone. I'm not the one threatening you. Who's been right so far? Who has the most to gain?

Remember, America: No matter what the problem, the squeaky wheel always gets the grease. You've got no excuse now. You're armed with the knowledge and confidence necessary to get through this. Have fun with these "tough guys" who will attempt to scare you into dealing with them.

Just go do it.

But play to win!

13

THE TOP 10 MOST FREQUENTLY ASKED QUESTIONS

"The only dumb question is the one not asked."
Anonymous

After all of the radio and television shows I've done over the last few years, it's easy to predict the most frequently asked questions. Some people miss some of the most important points the first time around, and I never want anyone out there to get caught in a trap just because something got by them. So here's my list of top ten questions . . . and answers!

QUESTION #1:

"Can the debt collectors call me at work?"

Yes, they can, so it's important to understand how to make them stop under federal law. If you tell the debt collector, "I cannot accept these types of calls at work . . . please do not call me here again," by law they must stop. Unfortunately, that doesn't mean they'll stop; your account may be passed around the debt collector's office from agent to agent, or they'll play dumb and say you never said that. Any way you look at it, you've got a problem if they're calling you.

Tell the debt collector that you can't take calls at work, but more importantly, follow this up immediately with a Cease & Desist letter modeled after the one in Appendix C

QUESTION #2:

"What if the debt collectors tell me that they are the only people I can deal with? I've heard them say that the original creditor won't work with me anymore and I must deal with them. Who is telling the truth?"

Oh, no—I hope you're sitting down. Are you ready? Okay . . . I've said this before and I'll say it again: Debt collectors sometimes lie! Hard to believe, until you understand that they're paid to collect past due accounts. It's real simple. If the original creditor wants to get paid, they'll deal with you . . . because that's the only person you're going to repay! Remember, you have the right under federal law NOT to deal with a debt collector. Since you're smart enough by now to hammer the debt collector with the Cease & Desist letter, and you are the one with the money, the original creditor won't have much of a choice if they want their money. End of discussion.

QUESTION #3:

"But the debt collector said he was the only one that can take any negative remarks off my credit reports! Now what do I do?"

I hope you're sitting down for this one, too. *A debt collector cannot remove the negative information placed on your report by the original creditor.* They can only control whatever remarks they themselves put on your report. If you're smart you won't engage in any conversations with them. Take them out with the Cease & Desist letter and deal only with the original creditor. The original creditor CAN remove all negative remarks that they have put on your report and any remarks placed there by their "hired gun" debt collectors. Trust me. I've seen countless creditors remove negative information from credit reports before . . . they'll do it for you if they want to get paid.

QUESTION #4:

"I finally talked with the original creditor about repaying this debt and they agreed to new terms, freezing the interest, not charging any more late fees and all of that, but they said they couldn't delete any negative information from my credit report. They said it was against federal law. Now what do I do?"

As hard as it may be to believe, sometimes individuals working at some of these large companies don't know much about federal laws. The Fair Credit Reporting Act basically says that all information reported must be correct. But nowhere does it state that all information must be reported. If the original creditor wants the money, make sure they agree to delete all negative information placed there by their company or their debt collector(s). If they don't agree up front in writing, you're wasting your time and money. Don't pay them unless they agree!

QUESTION #5:

"I've gotten a letter from an attorney that looks pretty threatening. How do I handle them?"

Any attorney who collects two or more debts a year is considered a debt collector under federal law and can be eliminated using the same Cease & Desist letter. Many attorneys make full use of their "impressive" titles and letterheads to intimidate consumers into paying them— a pretty lucrative business when you think about it. If the attorney is serious about suing you on the debt, they'll use their "one last contact" to let you know that this is the case. Then it's a judgment call for the consumer on whether or not to call their bluff . . . unless, of course, you're out of cash and couldn't pay them if you wanted to. Besides, just because they get a judgment doesn't mean they'll ever collect on it.

QUESTION #6:

"Should I get the creditor to just re-report the debt as "PAID AS AGREED" or remove it altogether?"

Definitely hold out for the total removal of any and all negative remarks placed on your reports by the original creditor or their debt collector(s). "PAID AS AGREED" smells of renegotiated repayments, and the credit community isn't stupid. If nothing is on your report, you're safe.

QUESTION #7:

"I keep reading about how wonderful Consumer Credit Counseling Service is. Their ads are compelling

and their sales pitch on the phone made sense. Why not let them handle the repayments and renegotiations of my debts."

Ask your new buddies at CCCS who pays them. Ask them if they receive ANY money from the creditor. Ask them who pays the bills. Wake up, Dorothy! You're *still* not back in Kansas! There are no free rides in this world. CCCS is a nonprofit organization, not a charity. They get a commission of 10-15% of the total monies they collect. Original creditors would much rather you repay your debts through CCCS because they would then only have to pay the smaller commission instead of 30-50% to Vito's Collection Agency. Remember, if CCCS is being paid by your creditors it stands to reason that their allegiance is to the creditors, not you. You know what really chaps my rear when it comes to CCCS? The way they've suckered in the national media with their propaganda machine. The truth is finally coming to the surface about their loyalties, and as long as you now know the truth, that's all that matters.

QUESTION #8:

"When you were on 'Donahue' a while back, the woman from the American Collectors Association said that just because you invoke federal law and repay the original creditor doesn't mean the debt collector won't get paid. She said they still receive their commission. Is that true?"

In many cases, yes. When a creditor assigns a portfo-

lio of debt to a collection agency the agreement usually
stipulates that the collection agency still receives their
commission even if the consumer repays the original
creditor. Should this matter to you? No. If the creditor
wants to continue to pay the debt collector for doing
nothing, that's their business. The fact is, the original
creditor is the only one that can clear all of the negative
comments off your credit reports. Think about this: If
more consumers flush the debt collectors with Cease &
Desist letters, how long will it be before the creditors
eliminate the debt collectors and handle long-term collections themselves? Think about it.

QUESTION #9:

*"Is there any chance the debt collector won't accept
my Cease & Desist letter? What do I do then?"*

Do you realize the volume of mail debt collection
agencies receive every day? Do you think the president
of the agency is out picking up the mail? Wrong! In
most cases a lower-level member of the clerical staff is
the one out picking up the mail or receiving it at their
offices. They'll sign for anything. They're used to it.

QUESTION #10:

*"What happens if I get a Certified Letter? Should I
sign for it? What happens if I don't? Don't I legally
have to?"*

Certified mail is a one-way street. Don't ever blindly
sign for it. Only two businesses routinely send out certified mail: Attorneys telling you they're planning on

suing you and debt collectors just threatening to. An attorney will usually send you a copy of the letter by regular first class mail in addition to the certified piece. If not, when you fail to pick up the certified letter and it's returned, they'll usually follow with the normal mail copy.

If you're on your rear you might as well make the opposition work for every inch they might gain on you. Don't be an easy target for their calls or correspondence. Don't sign for certified letters blindly. At the very least, check to see where they're coming from. If the letter carrier happens to catch you at home or at your post office box and attempt to deliver the certified letter to you, don't be afraid to refuse delivery. The postal worker doesn't work on commission, and could care less.

Appendix A
TOP 10 LIST OF CREDIT FACTS FOR CONSUMERS

1) Unless you live in a state with community property laws dictating division/claim of assets and liabilities, prospective creditors cannot inquire about your marital status. Furthermore, prospective creditors cannot inquire about your spouse's income, unless you are claiming both incomes to qualify for a loan.

2) Americans spend over 70% of their gross income every year repaying debt: home loans, auto loans and credit cards.

3) Age discrimination? The actuarial tables know for sure: In the "credit scoring" game, those individuals under the age of 25 score the lowest; prospective debtors in their forties score highest, and are most desirable to lend to in the eyes of the credit grantors.

4) Owning a home debt-free doesn't necessarily score any higher than owning one with a mortgage. However, the fact that you own your home scores positive points with a prospective creditor.

5) Be aware that if you are self-employed and applying for credit, this can subtract points in the credit scoring game because of inability to verify income, tenure, etc.

6) Credit card companies divide card users into three categories:

    a) "Revolvers"—those individuals that make the minimum payment each month;

b) "Average"—are those consumers that pay the balance off in full one month and the minimum balance the next; and

c) "Convenience users"—those consumers that pay the entire balance every month, thus avoiding interest charges (these are the least profitable to banks).

7) Over 70% of the consumers who use credit cards have no idea what interest rate they are paying on their cards.

8) Unless you have purchased a new car or home in the last 12 months, the chances of your seeing a recent credit report are 1 in 8.

9) Over 90% of Americans have no idea what their rights are under federal credit and collections laws.

10) Only 1 in 20 Americans has a current listing on file of all credit card account numbers to refer to in the event of theft or fraud.

Appendix B.1

Sample Letter to Obtain Free
Annual TRW Credit Report

JOHN RODY
3500 Maple Avenue, #1600
Dallas, TX 75219

February 1, 1995

TRW Consumer Assistance
P.O. Box 2350
Chatsworth, CA 91313-2350

RE: Free annual copy of my credit report

To Whom It May Concern:

Please forward a current copy of my credit report to my address listed above.

My date of birth is: 11-11-44.

My social security number is: 042-25-0000.

A photocopy of my driver's license is enclosed to confirm my identity.

Thank you for your prompt assistance in this matter.

Sincerely,

John Rody

JR:mib

Appendix B.2

Blank Sample Letter to Obtain Free Annual TRW Credit Report

_____
_____
_____

Date: _____

TRW Consumer Assistance
P.O. Box 2350
Chatsworth, CA 91313-2350

RE: Free annual copy of my credit report

To Whom It May Concern:

Please forward a current copy of my credit report to my address listed above.

My date of birth is: _____

My social security number is: _____

A photocopy of my driver's license is enclosed to confirm my identity.

Thank you for your prompt assistance in this matter.

Sincerely,

_____

Appendix B.3

Sample Letter To Obtain
CSC/Equifax Credit Report

FRANK DREBIN
150 N. Los Angeles St.
Los Angeles, CA 90012

September 2, 1995

Equifax Credit
P.O. Box 740241
Atlanta, GA 30374-0241

RE: Copy of my credit report

To Whom It May Concern:

Please forward a current copy of my credit report to my address listed above.

My date of birth is: 10-03-31.

My social security number is: 319-88-0000.

Enclosed is a money order in the amount of $8.00 to cover the associated costs.

Thank you for your prompt assistance in this matter.

Sincerely,

Frank Drebin

FD:ln

Appendix B.4

Blank Sample Letter To Obtain
CSC/Equifax Credit Report

_____

_____

_____

Date: _____

Equifax Credit
P.O. Box 740241
Atlanta, GA 30374-0241

RE: Copy of my credit report

To Whom It May Concern:

Please forward a current copy of my credit report to my address listed above.

My date of birth is: _____

My social security number is: _____

Enclosed is a money order in the amount of $8.00 to cover the associated costs.

Thank you for your prompt assistance in this matter.

Sincerely,

_____

Appendix B.5

Sample Letter To Obtain
TransUnion Credit Report

BILL GANNON
150 N. Los Angeles St.
Los Angeles, CA 90012

January 12, 1995

TransUnion
P.O. Box 7000
North Olmstead, OH 44070

RE: Copy of my credit report

To Whom It May Concern:

Please forward a current copy of my credit report to my address listed above.

My date of birth is: 09-31-29.

My social security number is: 556-23-3231.

Enclosed is a money order in the amount of $8.00 to cover the associated costs.

Thank you for your prompt assistance in this matter.

Sincerely,

Bill Gannon

BG:jf

Appendix B.6

Blank Sample Letter To Obtain
TransUnion Credit Report

_____

_____

_____

Date: _____

TransUnion
P.O. Box 7000
North Olmstead, OH 44070

RE: Copy of my credit report

To Whom It May Concern:

Please forward a current copy of my credit report to my address listed above.

My date of birth is: _____

My social security number is: _____

Enclosed is a money order in the amount of $8.00 to cover the associated costs.

Thank you for your prompt assistance in this matter.

Sincerely,

_____

Appendix C.1

Sample Cease & Desist Letter
Version #1

EDWARD HASKELL
323 Elm St.
Mayfield, NY 12117

<u>**CERTIFIED MAIL, RETURN RECEIPT REQUESTED # Z 123 456 789**</u>

February 29, 1995

Mr. Fred Rutherford
North American Collections Specialists
1313 Main Street, Suite 500
Mayfield, NY 12116

RE: <u>MasterCard account #5418 1234 5678 9101</u>

Dear Mr. Rutherford:

Greetings!

You are hereby notified under provisions of Public Laws 95-109 and 99-361, also known as the Fair Debt Collection Practices Act, that your services are no longer desired.

1) You and your organization must <u>CEASE & DESIST</u> all attempts to collect the above debt. Failure to comply with this law will result in my immediately filing a complaint with the Federal Trade Commission and this state's Attorney General's office. I will pursue all criminal and civil claims against you and your company.

2) Let this letter also serve as your warning that I may utilize telephone recording devices in order to document any telephone conversations that we may have in the future.

-- continued --

Mr. Fred Rutherford, *North America Collections Specialists*   **Page 2**
February 29, 1995

3) Furthermore, if any negative information is placed on my credit bureau reports by your agency after receipt of this notice, this will cause me to file suit against you and your organization, both personally and corporately, to seek any and all legal remedies available to me by law.

Since it is my policy neither to recognize nor deal with collection agencies, I intend to settle this account with the original creditor.

Have a nice day.

Sincerely,

Edward Haskell

EH:lr

Appendix C.2

Sample Cease & Desist Letter
Version #2

EDWARD HASKELL
323 Elm St.
Mayfield, NY 12117

CERTIFIED MAIL, RETURN RECEIPT REQUESTED # Z 123 456 789

February 29, 1995

Mr. Fred Rutherford
North American Collections Specialists
1313 Main Street, Suite 500
Mayfield, NY 12116

RE: MasterCard account #5418 1234 5678 9101

Dear Mr. Rutherford:

You are hereby notified under provisions of Public Laws 95-109 and 99-361, also known as the Fair Debt Collection Practices Act, that your services are no longer desired.

1) I am disputing the validity of this debt under the terms of the FDCPA, Section 809, a-c.

2) You and your organization must CEASE & DESIST all attempts to collect the above debt. Failure to comply with this law will result in my immediately filing a complaint with the Federal Trade Commission and this state's Attorney General's office. I will pursue all criminal and civil claims against you and your company.

-- continued --

Mr. Fred Rutherford, *North America Collections Specialists*   **Page 2**
February 29, 1995

3) Let this letter also serve as your warning that I may utilize telephone recording devices in order to document any telephone conversations that we may have in the future.

4) Furthermore, if any negative information is placed on my credit bureau reports by your agency after receipt of this notice, this will cause me to file suit against you and your organization, both personally and corporately, to seek any and all legal remedies available to me by law.

Since it is my policy neither to recognize nor deal with collection agencies, I intend to settle this account with the original creditor.

Have a nice day.

Sincerely,

Edward Haskell

EH:lr

Appendix C.3

Sample Cease & Desist Letter For
An Uncollectible/Unenforceable Debt

EDWARD HASKELL
323 Elm St.
Mayfield, NY 12117

<u>**CERTIFIED MAIL, RETURN RECEIPT REQUESTED # Z 123 456 789**</u>

February 29, 1995

Mr. Fred Rutherford
North American Collections Specialists
1313 Main Street, Suite 500
Mayfield, NY 12116

RE: <u>MasterCard account #5418 1234 5678 9101</u>

Dear Mr. Rutherford:

You are hereby notified under provisions of Public Laws 95-109 and 99-361, also known as the Fair Debt Collection Practices Act, that your services are no longer desired.

1) Since this debt is not enforceable due to the age of this account (it has been more than four years since I defaulted under the terms of the original agreement), I cannot be pursued civilly on this account.

2) You and your organization must <u>CEASE & DESIST</u> all attempts to collect the above debt. Failure to comply with this law will result in my immediately filing a complaint with the Federal Trade Commission and this state's Attorney General's office. I will pursue all criminal and civil claims against you and your company.

-- continued --

167

Mr. Fred Rutherford, *North America Collections Specialists*　　　**Page 2**
February 29, 1995

3) Let this letter also serve as your warning that I may utilize telephone recording devices in order to document any telephone conversations that we may have in the future.

4) Furthermore, if any negative information is placed on my credit bureau reports by your agency after receipt of this notice, this will cause me to file suit against you and your organization, both personally and corporately, to seek any and all legal remedies available to me by law.

Since it is my policy neither to recognize nor deal with collection agencies, I intend to settle this account with the original creditor.

Have a nice day.

Sincerely,

Edward Haskell

EH:lr

Appendix C.4

Blank Sample Cease & Desist Letter
Version #1

_____
_____
_____

CERTIFIED MAIL, RETURN RECEIPT REQUESTED #_____

Date: _____

_____
_____
_____
_____

RE: _____

Dear _____:

Greetings!

You are hereby notified under provisions of Public Laws 95-109 and 99-361, also known as the Fair Debt Collection Practices Act, that your services are no longer desired.

1) You and your organization must CEASE & DESIST all attempts to collect the above debt. Failure to comply with this law will result in my immediately filing a complaint with the Federal Trade Commission and this state's Attorney General's office. I will pursue all criminal and civil claims against you and your company.

-- continued --

_____ , _____   **Page 2**

_____

2) Let this letter also serve as your warning that I may utilize telephone recording devices in order to document any telephone conversations that we may have in the future.

3) Furthermore, if any negative information is placed on my credit bureau reports by your agency after receipt of this notice, this will cause me to file suit against you and your organization, both personally and corporately, to seek any and all legal remedies available to me by law.

Since it is my policy neither to recognize nor deal with collection agencies, I intend to settle this account with the original creditor.

Have a nice day.

Sincerely,

_____

Appendix C.5

Sample Cease & Desist Letter
Version #2

_____
_____
_____

<u>**CERTIFIED MAIL, RETURN RECEIPT REQUESTED #** _____</u>

Date: _____

_____
_____
_____
_____

RE: _____

Dear _____:

You are hereby notified under provisions of Public Laws 95-109 and 99-361, also known as the Fair Debt Collection Practices Act, that your services are no longer desired.

1) I am disputing the validity of this debt under the terms of the FDCPA, Section 809, a-c.

2) You and your organization must <u>CEASE & DESIST</u> all attempts to collect the above debt. Failure to comply with this law will result in my immediately filing a complaint with the Federal Trade Commission and this state's Attorney General's office. I will pursue all criminal and civil claims against you and your company.

-- continued --

_____ , _____   **Page 2**
_____

3) Let this letter also serve as your warning that I may utilize telephone recording devices in order to document any telephone conversations that we may have in the future.

4) Furthermore, if any negative information is placed on my credit bureau reports by your agency after receipt of this notice, this will cause me to file suit against you and your organization, both personally and corporately, to seek any and all legal remedies available to me by law.

Since it is my policy neither to recognize nor deal with collection agencies, I intend to settle this account with the original creditor.

Have a nice day.

Sincerely,

_____

Appendix C.6

Blank Cease & Desist Letter
For An Uncollectible/Unenforceable Debt

_____
_____
_____

<u>**CERTIFIED MAIL, RETURN RECEIPT REQUESTED #**</u> _____

Date: _____

_____
_____
_____

RE: <u>Account #</u> _____

Dear _____

You are hereby notified under provisions of Public Laws 95-109 and 99-361, also known as the Fair Debt Collection Practices Act, that your services are no longer desired.

1) Since this debt is not enforceable due to the age of this account (it has been more than _____ years since I defaulted under the terms of the original agreement), I cannot be pursued civilly on this account.

2) You and your organization must <u>CEASE & DESIST</u> all attempts to collect the above debt. Failure to comply with this law will result in my immediately filing a complaint with the Federal Trade Commission and this state's Attorney General's office. I will pursue all criminal and civil claims against you and your company.

-- continued --

_____, _____   **Page 2**

_____

3) Let this letter also serve as your warning that I may utilize telephone recording devices in order to document any telephone conversations that we may have in the future.

4) Furthermore, if any negative information is placed on my credit bureau reports by your agency after receipt of this notice, this will cause me to file suit against you and your organization, both personally and corporately, to seek any and all legal remedies available to me by law.

Since it is my policy not to recognize nor deal with collection agencies, I intend to settle this account with the original creditor.

Have a nice day.

Sincerely,

_____

Appendix D.1

HOW TO SEND
CERTIFIED MAIL

Using U.S. Postal Service Form #3800

STEP ONE: Fill in the first line (a) with the name of the Collection Agency.

STEP TWO: Fill in the second line (b) with the street or mailing address of the Collection Agency.

STEP THREE: Fill in the third line (c) with the city, state and zip code of the Collection Agency.

STEP FOUR: Attach the green label (bottom half) of the form directly to the upper left-hand corner of your envelope (to the right of your return address).

The Post Office will fill out the rest of the form after you have paid them the appropriate fee. Be sure to staple the white half of this form (your receipt) to your file copy of the letter you are about to send.

P 028 510 246

Receipt for Certified Mail
No Insurance Coverage Provided
Do not use for International Mail
(See Reverse)

ABC Collection Agency

P.O. BOX 12345

New York, NY 10010-245

Postage	$
Certified Fee	
Special Delivery Fee	
Restricted Delivery Fee	
Return Receipt Showing to Whom & Date Delivered	
Return Receipt Showing to Whom, Date, and Addressee's Address	
TOTAL Postage & Fees	$
Postmark or Date	

PS Form 3800, June 1991

Fold at line over top of envelope to the right of the return address.

CERTIFIED
P 028 510 246
MAIL

U.S. Postal Service Form #3800
- EXAMPLE -

175

U.S. Post Office Form #3811
(Green Return Reply/Receipt Card)

STEP ONE: Fill in your complete address (a)

STEP TWO: In section 3, fill in the name of the Collection Agency and the name of the representative to whom your letter is addressed. Be sure to include their zip code.

STEP THREE: In section 4a, fill in the number from U.S. Post Office Form #3800 (refer to Appendix D). Remember, this number should also be printed across the top of the letter being sent to the Collection Agency and representative.

STEP FOUR: In section 4b, mark the box with the word "Certified" next to it.

All of the other lines should be left blank. They will be filled in by the mail carrier delivering the letter to the Collection Agency and representative.

How To Correctly Complete U.S. Post Office Form #3811-A

Yellow Reply Card Tracer

This card is only filled out when it is apparent your green reply receipt card has been lost. Be sure to allow 14 days for the return of the green card.

Staple all of your receipts from when you originally mailed the letter to your file copy. You should have attached to your file copy of the letter you mailed the white half of U.S. Post Office Form #3800. When you mailed your letter, the Post Office filled in this part of the form, showing which services you requested and paid for, along with their postmark. This will give the postal clerk ample evidence to send this yellow tracer card through the system.

STEP ONE: Fill in your name and the same mailing/ return address you wrote on the green card (a).

STEP TWO: Fill in your city, state and zip code on this line (b). This will make sure this card is returned to your post office branch.

STEP THREE: Fill in the date you mailed your original letter on line 3. Use the date of the postmark on the white half of U.S. Postal Service Form #3800.

STEP FOUR: Fill in the "Certified No." of the letter you originally mailed on line 6. This number will be the same one printed at the top of the white half of U.S. Postal Service Form #3800 (referred to above).

STEP FIVE: Fill in the name and address of the Collection Agency where you sent your original letter on line 9. This name and address should match the one written on the white half of U.S. Postal Service Form #3800.

The postal clerk will handle the rest of the lines. You should receive this card within 14 days from the date you put in the tracer card.

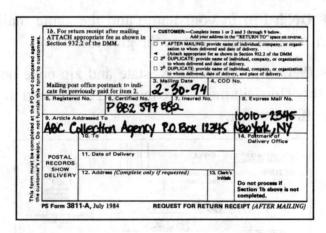

Appendix E.1

Sample Letter Utilized To Settle
An Outstanding Balance With A Creditor

MR. WARD CLEAVER
211 Pine Street
Mayfield, NY 12117

VIA CERTIFIED MAIL, RETURN RECEIPT REQUESTED #P 123 456 789

February 30, 1995

Mr. Richard Head
Vice President of Financial Services
Acme Department Store
1234 Disk Drive
Sonoffa Beach, CA 90010-1234

RE: Agreed settlement of outstanding balance of $725.00 on account #123-456

Dear Mr. Head:

As we have discussed through previous letters over the last few months, I am willing to settle the outstanding balance on my account referenced above.

By affixing your signature on this letter of settlement/agreement, you agree on behalf of Acme Department Stores, Inc. to the following:

1) You agree to accept a total of $72.50 as a final settlement of all outstanding charges/fees on the account referenced above. This will be paid to your company in certified funds as soon as I receive a signed and dated copy of this letter from you;

2) You agree to cease any and all attempts to collect this debt, either directly or through a Collection Agency;

--continued --

Mr. Richard Head, *Acme Department Store*   Page 2
February 29, 1995

3) You agree not to sell this debt to any third party since you now recognize this account to be "SETTLED AS AGREED";

4) You agree to retract **all** negative or derogatory remarks you may have reported on my credit report with any credit reporting agency located in the United States.

This agreement will not be binding until I receive a signed/dated original of this letter from you and in turn, I remit certified funds to your company, thus closing this transaction.

Please sign and return a copy of the letter enclosed in the attached pre-addressed/postage paid envelope.

Thank you for your cooperation in this matter.

Sincerely,   ACCEPTED AND AGREED TO:

Ward Cleaver   Richard Head   Date
WC:bs

Appendix E.2

Blank Sample Letter Format Utilized To Settle An Outstanding Balance With A Creditor

---

_____
_____
_____

<u>VIA CERTIFIED MAIL, RETURN RECEIPT REQUESTED #_____</u>

Date: _____

_____
_____
_____
_____

RE: Agreed settlement of outstanding balance of $_____ on account #_____

Dear _____:

As we have discussed through previous letters over the last few months, I am willing to settle the outstanding balance on my account referenced above.

By affixing your signature on this letter of settlement/agreement, you agree on behalf of ACME Department Stores, Inc. to the following:

1) You agree to accept a total of $_____ as a final settlement of all outstanding charges/fees on the account referenced above. This will be paid to your company in certified funds as soon as I receive a signed and dated copy of this letter from you;

2) You agree to cease any and all attempts to collect this debt, either directly or through a Collection Agency;

-- continued --

_____ , _____   **Page 2**
_____

3) You agree not to sell this debt to any third party since you now recognize this account to be "SETTLED AS AGREED";

4) You agree to retract **all** negative or derogatory remarks you may have reported on my credit report with any credit reporting agency located in the United States.

This agreement will not be binding until I receive a signed/dated original of this letter from you and in turn, I remit certified funds to your company, thus closing this transaction.

Please sign and return a copy of the letter enclosed in the attached pre-addressed/postage paid envelope.

Thank you for your cooperation in this matter.

Sincerely,   ACCEPTED AND AGREED TO:

_____   _____
                            Signature   Printed Name   Date

Appendix F.1

Sample "See You In Bankruptcy Court" Letter Utilized To Renegotiate An Outstanding Balance With A Creditor

MS. JUNE CLEAVER
211 Pine Street
Mayfield, NY 12117

VIA CERTIFIED MAIL, RETURN RECEIPT REQUESTED #P 123 456 789

February 30, 1995

Mr. Richard Head
Vice President of Credit Card Services
First National Bank of Mayfield
6900 Grant Ave., Suite 1100
Mayfield, NY 12115

RE: Account #321-567

Dear Mr. Head:

I am writing to you directly in hopes of getting my financial situation with your bank back under control and resolved quickly and amicably.

Due to a series of unexpected events, my financial situation has deteriorated to the point that I have consulted with an attorney about filing a Chapter 7 bankruptcy petition.

With the interest rate and late fees being assessed by your bank (and others), I am unable to make any meaningful progress in amortizing the debt. I cannot and will not continue to "borrow from Peter to pay Paul."

I really hope to avoid bankruptcy reorganization and feel that, with your assistance, I will be able to work something out to everybody's benefit.

-- continued --

Mr. Richard Head, *First National Bank of Mayfield*   Page 2
February 30, 1995

I would like to enter into an agreement that would freeze the current balance of $3,000 and allow me to make 20 consecutive payments of $150 each. Furthermore, once I have successfully repaid this debt as outlined, you agree to cause any and all negative remarks reported by your organization or any debt collection agency you have employed removed from all of my credit bureau reports in the United States.

I cannot spend time or money sending you counter proposals. Let's agree on this repayment plan or one that you may propose that reaches the same goals quickly, or else I will be forced to file my petition with the federal courts.

I look forward to your prompt written reply.

Sincerely,

signature

June Cleaver

Appendix F.2

Blank "See You In Bankruptcy Court" Letter Utilized To Renegotiate An Outstanding Balance With A Creditor

---

_____
_____
_____

VIA CERTIFIED MAIL, RETURN RECEIPT REQUESTED #_____

Date: _____

_____
_____
_____
_____

RE: Account #_____

Dear _____:

I am writing to you directly in hopes of getting my financial situation with your bank back under control and resolved quickly and amicably.

Due to a series of unexpected events, my financial situation has deteriorated to the point that I have consulted with an attorney about filing a Chapter 7 bankruptcy petition.

With the interest rate and late fees being assessed by your bank (and others), I am unable to make any meaningful progress in amortizing the debt. I cannot and will not continue to "borrow from Peter to pay Paul."

I really hope to avoid bankruptcy reorganization and feel that, with your assistance, I will be able to work something out to everybody's benefit.

-- continued --

_____ , _____   **Page 2**

_____

I would like to enter into an agreement that would freeze the current balance of $_____ and allow me to make _____ consecutive payments of $_____ each. Furthermore, once I have successfully repaid this debt as outlined, you agree to cause any and all negative remarks reported by your organization or any debt collection agency you have employed removed from all of my credit bureau reports in the United States.

I cannot spend time or money sending you counter proposals. Let's agree on this repayment plan or one that you may propose that reaches the same goals quickly, or else I will be forced to file my petition with the federal courts.

I look forward to your prompt written reply.

Sincerely,

_____

Appendix G.1

Sample Letter For Corresponding To
The Department Of Education

OPIE TAYLOR
14 Maple Street
Mayberry NC 27611

<u>**VIA CERTIFIED MAIL, RETURN RECEIPT REQUESTED #P 100 009 436**</u>

September 31, 1994

U.S. Department of Education
ATTN: Student Loan Workouts
7th and D Streets, Room 5102
Washington, D.C. 20202

RE: Account #S246-10-0000

To Whom It May Concern:

I need to restructure my outstanding student loan (my account number is referenced above).

It is my understanding that under the Student Loan Reform Act (Public Law 103-66) there are several options available to me. I wish to get this situation restructured and under control as soon as possible.

Please forward all applications and paperwork to my attention at the address listed at the top of this page, as soon as possible. I wish to establish a repayment plan immediately.

Sincerely,

Opie

Opie Taylor

Appendix G.2

Blank Letter For Corresponding To
The Department Of Education

         _____

         _____

         _____

VIA CERTIFIED MAIL, RETURN RECEIPT REQUESTED # _____

Date: _____

U.S. Department of Education
ATTN: Student Loan Workouts
7th and D Streets, Room 5102

Washington, D.C. 20202

RE: Account # _____

To Whom It May Concern:

I need to restructure my outstanding student loan (my account number is referenced above).

It is my understanding that under the Student Loan Reform Act (Public Law 103-66) there are several options available to me. I wish to get this situation restructured and under control as soon as possible.

Please forward all applications and paperwork to my attention at the address listed at the top of this page, as soon as possible. I wish to establish a repayment plan immediately.

Sincerely,

_____

Appendix H

Sample Letter Sent To Automobile Lease/Finance Company

DAVE TANNER
3500 Maple Avenue, #1600
Dallas, TX 75219

CERTIFIED MAIL, RETURN RECEIPT REQUESTED # R 123 456 789

February 29, 1995

Mr. Fred Rutherford
Mayfield AutoLease
3939 Wall Street, Suite 1600
Mayfield, NY 12116

RE: Account #5678 6900 9101

Dear Mr. Rutherford:

Due to financial circumstances beyond my control, I will be unable to fulfill the terms of my automobile lease originated by your company on April 1, 1993. I would like to propose the following:

1) I return the car to you or your authorized agent in clean condition by end of business on March 15, 1994.

2) As a result of this voluntary repossession, you will be forced to sell the car at auction. I would appreciate your notifying me of the price the car brought at the auction, along with the deficiency balance owed to your company.

-- continued --

Mr. Fred Rutherford, *Mayfield AutoLease*   **Page 2**
February 29, 1995

3) As soon as my financial situation stabilizes I'd like to begin repaying this balance, with the understanding that once I have repaid the amount owed, your company will remove all negative information regarding this account from all credit bureau files.

4) Furthermore, since I am voluntarily turning the car back over to your company, you agree not to pursue any collection either in-house or through a third-party debt collector.

If you agree to the terms I have outlined in this letter, please sign and date a copy and return to me at the mailing address listed above.

I appreciate your assistance and prompt written reply in this matter.

Sincerely,   AGREED AND ACCEPTED

Dave Tanner   Signature   Printed Name   Date

Appendix I.1

Sample Complaint Letter To
The Federal Trade Commission

CHIN HO KELLY
2565 Mauna Kea Place
Honolulu, HI 96820

April 26, 1995

Federal Trade Commission
450 Golden Gate Avenue, Room 12470
San Francisco, CA 94102

To Whom It May Concern:

I am having difficulties with several companies and request that you immediately send to me all of the appropriate forms to file complaints with your agency about the violations of the following two federal laws:

> The Fair Debt Collections Practices Act
> The Fair Credit Reporting Act

I look forward to your prompt reply.

Sincerely,

Chin Ho Kelly

CHK:gf

Appendix I.2

Blank Sample Complaint Form Letter
To The Federal Trade Commission

_____
_____
_____

Date: _____

Federal Trade Commission

_____
_____

To Whom It May Concern:

I am having difficulties with several companies and request that you immediately send to me all of the appropriate forms to file complaints with your agency about the violations of the following two federal laws:

The Fair Debt Collections Practices Act
The Fair Credit Reporting Act

I look forward to your prompt reply.

Sincerely,

_____

Appendix I.3

Blank Sample Complaint Letter Format
To The State Attorney General's Office

_____
_____
_____

Date: _____

Consumer Protection Division
State of _____ Attorney General's Office
_____

To Whom It May Concern:

I am being harassed by several debt collection agencies and request that you immediately send to me all of the appropriate forms so that I may file a complaint with your agency about violations of the following two federal laws:

> The Fair Debt Collections Practices Act
> The Fair Credit Reporting Act

I am sure the actions of these debt collectors must be in violation of various state consumer protection law statutes as well. Please send me the necessary paperwork so that I may take action against these individuals and their companies.

I look forward to your prompt reply.

Sincerely,

_____

Appendix J.1
Federal Trade Commission Regional

Federal Trade Commission Headquarters
6th & Pennsylvania Avenue, NW
Washington, DC 20580
(202) 326-2222

Federal Trade Commission
1718 Peachtree St., NW, Room 1000
Atlanta, GA 30367
(404) 347-4836

(covers Alabama, Florida, Georgia, Mississippi,
North Carolina, South Carolina, Tennessee & Virginia)

Federal Trade Commission
10 Causeway St., Suite 1184
Boston, MA 02222-1073
(617) 565-7240

(covers Connecticut, Maine, Massachusetts,
New Hampshire, Rhode Island & Vermont)

Federal Trade Commission
55 E. Monroe St., Suite 1437
Chicago, IL 60603
(312) 353-4423

(covers Illinois, Indiana, Iowa, Kentucky,
Minnesota, Missouri & Wisconsin)

Federal Trade Commission
668 Euclid Avenue, Suite 520-A
Cleveland, OH 44114
(216) 522-4207

(covers Delaware, Maryland, Michigan,
Ohio, Pennsylvania & West Virginia)

Federal Trade Commission
100 North Central Expressway, Suite 500
Dallas, TX 75201-4396
(214) 767-5501
(covers Arkansas, Louisiana, New Mexico, Oklahoma & Texas)

Federal Trade Commission
1405 Curtis St., Suite 2900
Denver, CO 80202
(303) 844-2271
(covers Colorado, Kansas, Montana, Nebraska,
North Dakota, South Dakota, Utah & Wyoming)

Federal Trade Commission
11000 Wilshire Blvd.
Los Angeles, CA 90024
(310) 575-7575
(covers Arizona & Southern California)

Federal Trade Commission
150 William Street, Suite 1300
New York, NY 10038
(212) 264-1207
(cover New Jersey & New York)

Federal Trade Commission
901 Market Street, Suite 570
San Francisco, CA 94103
(415) 744-7920
(covers northern California, Hawaii & Nevada)

Federal Trade Commission
2806 Federal Building
915 Second Avenue
Seattle, WA 98174
(206) 220-6363
(covers Alaska, Idaho, Oregon & Washington)

Appendix K
Resources Reference List

Bankcard Holders of America: Want to find the best deal on low interest bank or credit cards? These are the people to contact. Write to them at 560 Herndon Parkway, Suite 120, Herndon, VA 22070. Here's their number to reach them: (703) 389-5445.

Consumer Fresh Start: If you've already committed the cardinal sin of personal finance and have filed for or emerged from a personal bankruptcy, this consumer group provides counseling, support and most importantly ideas on how to get back on your feet. Their address is 217 N. Church Street, Princeton, IL 61356.

American Collector's Association (ACA): I don't have an enormous amount of faith in this trade association designed to "self-police" the debt collection industry. They'll investigate complaints from consumers, but my best advice is to complain first to the Federal Trade Commission and your state's Attorney General, with a copy of your letters and official complaint copied to the ACA. (While you're at it, send a copy to me, too. Send it to my attention, in care of the publisher. Their address is listed in the front of the book.) Here's the address for the ACA: Post Office Box 35106, Minneapolis, MN 55435.

Consumer Resource Handbook: Published by the U.S. Office of Consumer Affairs, this book is definitely worth the price (free!) and has listings of hundreds of agencies that are there to help consumers with a variety of problems. To get your free copy, write to: The Consumer Resource Handbook, Pueblo, CO 81009.

Debtors Anonymous: Support groups can be invaluable in your desire to keep on track financially. Write to Debtors Anonymous at P.O. Box 400, Grand Central Station, New York, NY 10163 to find out if there is a chapter near you.

Remember, *the squeaky wheel gets the grease.* If one of these credit card companies is making your life miserable and you really don't deserve it, start at the top! Call the company in question first to find out the name of the chairman or president (these things change, you know) and send them a certified letter. Results is the name of the game. Persistence does pay. Here's the top four national consumer credit/charge card company addresses:

American Express
American Express Tower
World Financial Center
200 Vesey St
New York, NY 10285
(212) 640-2000

Discover Card Services, Inc.
2500 Lake Cook Road, Suite 2-C
Riverwood, IL 60015
(708) 405-0900

MasterCard USA
888 Seventh Avenue
New York, NY 10106
(212) 649-4600

VISA USA, Inc.
3155 Clearview Way
San Mateo, CA 94402
(415) 570-3200

Appendix L

Facts for Consumers About Fair Credit Billing Practices
from the Federal Trade Commission
September 1992

Fair Credit Billing

Has the department store's computer billed you for merchandise you returned to the store or never received? Or has a credit card company ever charged you twice for the same item or failed to properly credit a payment made on your account? Credit billing errors do occur, but they are easy to resolve if you know how to use the Fair Credit Billing Act (FCBA). Congress passed this law in 1975 to help consumers resolve disputes with creditors and to ensure fair handling of credit accounts.

Which credit transactions are covered?

The FCBA generally applies only to "open end" credit accounts. Open end accounts include credit card, revolving charge accounts (such as department store accounts) and overdraft checking. The periodic bills, or billing statements, you receive (usually monthly) for such accounts are covered by the FCBA. The Act does not apply to a load or credit sale which is paid according to a fixed schedule until the entire amount is paid back.

What types of disputes are covered?

The FCBA settlement procedure applies only to disputes over "billing errors" on periodic statements, such as the following:
- Charges not made by you or anyone authorized to use your account.
- Charges which are incorrectly identified or for which the wrong amount or date is shown.

• Charges for goods or services you did not accept or which were not delivered as agreed.

• Computational or similar errors.

• Failure to properly reflect payments or other credits, such as returns.

• Not mailing or delivering bills to your current address (provided you give a change of address at least 20 days before the billing period ends).

• Charges for which you request an explanation or written proof of purchase.

How to use the settlement procedure

When many consumers find a mistake on their bill, they pick up the phone and call the company to correct the problem. You can do this if you wish, but phoning does not trigger the legal safeguards provided under the FCBA.

To be protected under the law, you must send a separate written billing error notice to the creditor. Your notice must reach the creditor within 60 days after the first bill containing the error was mailed to you. Send the notice to the address provided on the bill for billing error notices (and not, for example, directly to the store, unless the bill says that's where it should be sent). In your letter, you must include the following information:

• Your name and account number.

• A statement that you believe the bill contains a billing error and the dollar amount involved.

• The reasons why you believe there is a mistake.

It's a good idea to send it by certified mail, with a return receipt requested. That way you'll have proof of the dates of mailing and receipt. If you wish, send photocopies of sales slips or other documents, but keep the originals for your records.

What must the creditor do?

Your letter claiming a billing error must be acknowledged by the creditor in writing *within 30 days* after it is received, unless the problem is resolved within that period. In any case, within two billing cycles (but not more than 90 days), the creditor *must* conduct a reasonable investigation and either correct the mistake or explain why the bill is believed to be correct.

What happens while a bill is being disputed?

You may withhold payment of the amount in dispute, including the affected portions of minimum payments and finance charges, until the dispute is resolved. You are still required to pay any part of the bill which is not disputed, including finance and other charges on undisputed amounts.

While the FCBA dispute settlement procedure is going on, the creditor may not take any legal or other action to collect the amount in dispute. Your account may not be closed or restricted in any way, except that the disputed amount may be applied against your credit limit.

What about your credit rating?

While a bill is being disputed, the creditor may not threaten to damage your credit rating or report you as delinquent to anyone. However, the creditor is permitted to report that you are disputing your bill.

Another federal law, the Equal Credit Opportunity Act, prohibits creditors from discriminating against credit applicants who, in good faith, exercise their rights under the FCBA. You cannot be denied credit merely because you have disputed a bill.

If the creditor makes a mistake

If your bill is found to contain a billing error, the creditor must write you explaining the corrections to be made on your account. In addition to crediting your account with the amount not owed, the creditor must remove all finance charges, late fees, or other charges relating to that amount. If the creditor concludes that you owe part of the disputed amount, this must be explained in writing. You also have the right to request copies of documents proving you owe the money.

If the bill is correct

If the creditor investigates and still believes the bill is correct, you must be told promptly in writing how much you owe and why. You may also ask for copies of relevant documents. At this point, you will owe the disputed amount, plus any finance charges that accumulated while it was disputed. You may also have to pay the minimum payment amount missed because of the dispute.

If you still disagree

Even after the FCBA dispute settlement procedure has ended, you may still feel the bill is wrong. If this happens, *write* the creditor *within 10 days* after receiving the explanation and say you still refuse to pay the disputed amount. At this point, the creditor may begin collection procedures. However, if the creditor reports you to a credit bureau as delinquent, he must also state that you don't think you owe the money. Also, you must be told who receives such reports.

If the creditor doesn't follow the procedures

Any creditor who fails to follow the FCBA dispute settlement procedure may not collect the amount in dispute, or any finance charges on it, up to $50, *even if the bill turns out to be correct*. For example, this penalty would apply if a creditor acknowledges your complaint in 45 days (15 days too late) or takes more than two billing cycles to resolve a dispute. It also applies if a creditor threatens to report—or goes ahead and improperly reports—your nonpayments to anyone. You also have the right, as more fully described below, to sue a creditor for any violation of the FCBA.

Complaints about quality

Disputes about the quality of goods and services are not necessarily "billing errors," so the dispute procedure may not apply. However, if you purchase unsatisfactory goods or services with a credit card, the FCBA allows you to take the same legal actions against the credit card issuer as you could take under state law against the seller. If your state law permits you to withhold payment to a seller for defective merchandise, or pay and sue for a refund, you might also be able to withhold payment to your credit card issuer. Because state laws on your right to stop payment vary, it is best to get legal advice before you do so.

However, before you take legal action, you must give the seller a chance to remedy the problem. Also, unless the seller is also the card issuer (such as a company that issued you a gasoline credit card), you must have bought the item in your home state or within 100 miles of your current mailing address, and the amount charged must have been more than $50.

Other billing rights for consumers

The FCBA also requires "open end" creditors to do the following for their customers:

• Give you a written notice when you open a new account, and at other specified times, describingyour right to dispute billing errors.

• Provide a statement for each billing period in which you owe or they owe you more that $1.00.

• Mail or deliver your bill to you at least 14 days before the payment is due, if you are given a time period within which to pay the bill without incurring additional finance or other charges.

• Credit all payments to your account as of the date they are received, unless not doing so would not result in extra charges.

• Promptly credit or refund overpayments.

You can also sue

You can sue a creditor who violates any FCBA provisions. If you win, you may be awarded damages resulting from the violation, plus *twice the amount* of any finance charge (not less than $100 or more than $1,000). The court may also order the creditor to pay your attorney's fees and costs. If possible, retain a private attorney who is willing to accept whatever fee the court awards as the entire fee to representing you. Some lawyers may not be willing to accept your case unless you agree to pay their fee—win or lose—or if you will add to a fee awarded by the court but which they believe is too low. Be sure you get a full explanation of what it could cost before you go to court.

Where to report FCBA violations

The Federal Trade Commission enforces the FCBA for almost all creditors except banks. While the Commission does not represent individuals in private disputes, information from consumers as to their experiences and concerns is vital to the enforcement of the Act. Questions or complaints may be addressed to the nearest Federal Trade Commission Regional Office. If they concern national creditors, write:

Federal Trade Commission,
Fair Credit Billing, Washington, D.C. 20580

Appendix M

The Fair Debt Collection Practices

PUBLIC LAW 95-109   SEPT. 20, 1977

CONSUMER CREDIT PROTECTION ACT, AMENDMENTS

FAIR DEBT COLLECTION PRACTICES ACT
As Amended by Public Law 99-361 - July 9, 1986

PUBLIC LAW 95-109
95TH CONGRESS

An Act

Sept. 20, 1977
(H.R. 5294)

To amend the Consumer Credit Protection Act to prohibit abusive practices by debt collectors.

Consumer Credit Protection Act, amendments.

Be it enacted by the Senate and House of Representatives of the United States of America in Congress assembled, That the Consumer Credit Protection Act (15 U.S.C. 1601 et seq.) is amended by adding at the end thereof the following new title:

Fair Debt Collection Practices Act

"TITLE VIII—DEBT COLLECTION PRACTICES

"Sec.

"801. Short Title.

"802. Findings and purpose.

"803. Definitions.

"804. Acquisition of location information.

"805. Communication in connection with debt collection.

"806. Harassment or abuse.

"807. False or misleading representations.

"808. Unfair practices.

"809. Validation of debts.

"810. Multiple debts.

"811. Legal actions by debt collectors.

"812. Furnishing certain deceptive forms.

"813. Civil liability.

"814. Administrative enforcement.

"815. Reports by Congress by the Commission.

"816. Relation to State laws.

"817. Exemption for State regulation.

"818. Effective date.

15 USC 1601
note

§ "801. Short Title

"This title may be cited as the 'Fair Debt Collection Practices Act'.

15 USC 1692

§ "802. Findings and purpose

"(a) There is abundant evidence of the use of abusive, deceptive, and unfair debt collection practices by many debt collectors. Abusive debt collection practices contribute to the number of personal bankruptcies, to marital instability,, to the loss of jobs, and to invasions of individual privacy.

"(b) Existing laws and procedures for redressing these injuries are in adequate to protect consumers.

"(c) Means other than misrepresentation or other abusive debt collection practice are available for the effective collection of debts.

"(d) Abusive debt collection practices are carried on to a substantial extent in interstate commerce and through means and instrumentalities of such commerce. Even where abusive debt collection practices are purely intrastate in character, they nevertheless directly affect interstate commerce.

"(e) It is the purpose of this title to eliminate abusive debt collection practices by debt collectors, to insure that those debt collectors who refrain from using abusive debt collection practices are not competitively disadvantaged, and to promote consistent State action to protect consumers against debt collection abuses.

15 USC 1692a.

§ "803. Definitions

"As used in this title—

"(1) The term "Commission" means the Federal Trade Commission.

"(2) The term "communication" means the conveying of information regarding a debt directly or indirectly to any person through any medium.

"(3) The term "consumer" means any natural person obligated or allegedly obligated to pay any debt.

"(4) The term "creditor" means nay person who offers or extends credit creating a debt or to whom a debt is owed, but such term does not include any person to the extent that he receives an assignment or transfer of a debt in default solely for the purpose of facilitating collection of such debt for another.

"(5) The term "debt" means any obligation or alleged obligation of a consumer to pay money arising out of a transaction in which the money, property, insurance, or services which are the subject of the transaction are primarily for personal, family, or household purposes, whether or not such obligation has been reduces to judgment.

"(6) The term "debt collector" means any person who uses any instrumentality of interstate commerce or the mails in any business the principal purpose of which is the collection of any debts, or who regularly collects or attempts to collect, directly or indirectly, debts owed or due or asserted to be owed or due another. Notwithstanding the exclusion provided by clause (F) of the last sentence of the paragraph, the term includes any creditor who, in the process of collecting his own debts, uses any name other than his own which would indicate that a third person is collecting or attempting to collect such debts. For the purpose of Section 808(6), such term also includes any person who uses any instrumentality of interstate commerce or the mails in any business the principal purpose of which is the enforcement of security interests. The term does not include -

"(A) any officer or employee of a creditor while, in the name of the creditor, collecting debts for such creditor;

"(B) any person while acting as a debt collector for another person, both of whom are related by common ownership or affiliated by corporated control, if the person acting as a debt collector does so only for persons to who it is so related or affiliated and if the principal business of such person is no the collection of debts;

"(C) any officer of employee of the United States or any State to the extent that collecting or attempting to collect any debt is in the performance of his official duties;

"(D) any person while serving or attempting to serve legal process on any other person in connection with the judicial enforcement of any debt;

"(E) any nonprofit organization which, at the request of consumers, performs bona fide consumer credit counseling and assists consumers in the liquidation of their debts by receiving payments form such consumers and distributing such amounts to creditors; and

"(F) any person collecting or attempting o collect any debt owed or due or asserted to be owed or due another to the extent such activity (i) is incidental to a bona fide fiduciary obligation or a bona fide escrow arrangement; (ii) concerns a debt which was originated by such person; (iii) concerns a debt which was not in default at the time it was obtained by such person as a secured party in a commercial credit transaction involving the creditor.

"(7) The term "location information" means a consumer's place of abode and his telephone number at such place, or his place of employment.

"(8) The tern "State" means any State, territory, or possession of the United States, the District of Columbia, the Commonwealth of Puerto Rico, or and political subdivision of any of the foregoing.

15 USC 1692b. § **" 804. Acquisition of location information**
"Any debt collector communicating with any person other than the consumer for the purpose of acquiring location information about the consumer shall-

"(1) identify himself, state that he is confirming or correcting location information concerning the consumer, and, only if expressly requested, identify his employer;

"(2) not state that such consumer owed any debt;

"(3) not communicate with any such person more than once unless requested to do so by such person or unless the debt collector reasonably believes that the earlier response of such person is erroneous or incomplete and that such person now has correct or complete location information;

"(4) not communicate by post card;

"(5) not use any language or symbol on any envelope or in the contents of an communication effected by the mails or telegram that indicated that the debt collector is in the debt collection business or that the communication relates to the collection of a debt; and

"(6) after the debt collector knows the consumer is represented by an attorney with regard to the subject debt and has knowledge of, or can readily ascertain, such attorney's name and address, not communicate with any person other than that attorney, unless the attorney fails to respond with a reasonable period of time to communication from the debt collector.

15 USC 1692c. § " **805 Communication in connection with debt collection**

(a) COMMUNICATION WITH THE CONSUMER GENERALLY.-Without the prior consent of the consumer given directly to the debt collector or the express permission of a court of competent jurisdiction, a debt collector may not communicate with a consumer in connection with the collection of any debt-

"(1) at any unusual time of place or a time or place known or which should be known to be inconvenient to the consumer. In the absence of knowledge of circumstances to the contrary, a debt collector shall assume that the convenient time for communicating with a consumer is after 8 o'clock antimeridian and before 9 o'clock postmeridian, local time at the consumer's location;

"(2) if the debt collector knows the consumer is represented by an attorney with respect to such debt and has knowledge of, or can readily ascertain, such attorney's name and address, unless the attorney fails to respond within a reasonable period of time to a communication from the debt collector or unless the attorney consents to direct communication with the consumer; or

"(3) at the consumer's place of employment if the debt collector knows or has reason to know that the consumer's employer prohibits the consumer from receiving such communication.

"(b) COMMUNICATION WITH THIRD PARTIES.- Except as provided in section 804, without the prior consent of the consumer given directly to the debt collector, or the express permission of a court of competent jurisdiction, or as reasonable necessary to effectuate a postjudgement judicial remedy, a debt collector may not communicate, in connection with the collection of any debt, with any person other than the consumer, his attorney, a consumer reporting agency if otherwise permitted by law, the creditor, the attorney of the creditor, or the attorney of the debt collector.

"(c) CEASING COMMUNICATION.- If a consumer notifies a debt collector in writing that the consumer refuses to pay a debt or that the consumer wishes the debt collector to cease further communication with the consumer, the debt collector shall not communicate further with the consumer with respect to such debt, except-

"(1) to advise the consumer that the debt collector's further efforts are being terminated;

"(2) to notify the consumer that the debt collector or creditor may invoke specified remedies which are ordinarily invoked by such debt collector or creditor; or

"(3 where applicable, to notify the consumer that the debt collector or creditor intends to invoke a specified remedy. If such notice from the consumer is made by mail, notification shall be complete upon receipt.

"(d) For the purpose of the section, the term "consumer" includes the consumer's spouse, parent (if the consumer is a minor), guardian, executor, or administrator.

15 USC 1692d

§ " **806. Harassment or abuse**

"A debt collector may not engage in any conduct the natural consequence of which is to harass, oppress, or abuse any person in connection with the collection of a debt. Without limiting the general application of the foregoing, the following conduct is a violation of this section:

"(1) The use or threat of use of violence or other criminal means to harm the physical person, reputation, or property of any person.

"(2) The use of obscene or profane language or language the natural consequence of which is to abuse the hearer or reader.

"(3) The publication of a list of consumers who allegedly refuse to pay debts, except to a consumer reporting agency or to persons meeting the requirements of section 603(f) or 604(3) of the Act.

"(4) The advertisement for sale of any debt to coerce payment of the debt.

"(5) Causing a telephone to ring or engaging any person in telephone conversation repeatedly or continuously with intent to annoy, abuse, or harass any person at the called number.

"(6) Except as provided in section 804, the placement of telephone calls without meaningful disclosure of the caller's identity.

15 USC 1692e.

§ " **807. False or misleading representations**

"A debt collector may not use any false, deceptive, or misleading representation or means in connection with the collection of any debt. Without limiting the general application of the foregoing, the following conduct is a violation of this section:

"(1) The false representation or implication that the debt collector is vouched for, bonded by, or affiliated with the United States of any State, including the use of any badge, uniform, or facsimile thereof.

"(2) The false representation of-

"(A) the character, amount, or legal status of any debt; or

"(B) any services rendered or compensation which may be lawfully received by any debt collector for the collection of a debt.

"(3) The false representation or implication that any individual is an attorney or that any communications is from an attorney.

"(4) The representation or implication that nonpayment of any debt will result in the arrest or imprisonment of any person or the seizure, garnishment, attachment, or sale of any property or wages of any per son unless such action is lawful and the debt collector or creditor intends to take such action.

"(5) The threat to take any action that cannot legally be taken or that is not intended to be taken.

"(6) The false misrepresentation or implication that a sale, referral, or other transfer of any interest in a debt shall cause the consumer to-

"(A) lose any claim or defense to payment of the debt or;

"(B) become subject to any practice prohibited by this title.

"(7) The false representation or implication that the consumer committed any crime or other conduct in order to disgrace the consumer.

"(8) Communicating or threatening to communicate to any person credit information which is known or which should be known to be false, including the failure to communicate that a disputed debt is disputed.

"(9) The use or distribution of any written communication which simulates or is falsely represented to be a document authorized, issued, or approved by any court, official, or agency of the United States or any State, or which creates a false impressions as to its source, authorization, or approval.

"(10) The use of any false representation or deceptive means to collect or attempt to collect any debt or to obtain information concerning a consumer.

"(11) Except as otherwise provided for communications to acquire location information under section 804, the failure to disclose clearly in all communications made to collect a debt or to obtain information about a consumer, that the debt collector is attempting to collect a debt and that any information obtained will be used for that purpose.

"(12) The false representation or implication that accounts have been turned over to innocent purchasers for value.

"(13) The false misrepresentation or implication that documents are legal process.

"(14) The use of any business, company, or organization name other than the true name of the debt collector's business, company or organization.

"(15) The false representation or implication that documents are not legal process forms or do not require action by the consumer.

"(16) The false representation or implication that a debt collector operates or is employed by a consumer reporting agency as defined by section 603(f) of the Act.

15 USC 1692f.

§ " **808. Unfair practices**

"A debt collector may not use unfair or unconscionable means to collect or attempt to collect any debt. Without limiting the general application of the foregoing, the following conduct is a violation of this section:

"(1) The collection of any amount (including interest, fee, charge, or expense incidental to the principal obligation) unless such amount is expressly authorized by the agreement creating the debt or permitted by law.

"(2) The acceptance by a debt collector from any person of a check or other payment instrument postdated by more than five days unless such person is notified in writing of the debt collector's intent to deposit such check or instrument not more than ten nor less than three business days prior to such deposit.

"(3) The solicitation by a debt collector of any postdated check or other postdated payment instrument for the purpose of threatening or instituting criminal prosecution.

"(4) Depositing or threatening to deposit and postdated check or other postdated payment instrument prior to the date on such check or instrument.

"(5) Causing charges to be made to any person for communications be concealment of the true purpose of the communication. Such charges include, but are not limited to, collect telephone calls and telegram fees.

"(6) Taking or threatening to take any nonjudicial action to effect dispossession of disablement of proper if-

"(A) there is no present right to possession of the proper; or

"(B) there is no present intention to take possession of the proper; or

"(C) The proper is exempt by law from such dispossession or disablement.

"(7) Communicating with a consumer regarding a debt by post card.

"(8) Using any language or symbol, other than the debt collector's address, on any envelope when communicating with a consumer by use of the mails or by telegram, except that a debt collector may use his business name if such name does not indicate that he is in the collection business.

15 USC 1692g.

§ " **809. Validation of debts**

"(a) Within five days after the initial communication with a consumer in connection with the collection of any debt, a debt collector shall, unless the following information is contained in the initial communication or the consumer has paid the debt, send the consumer a written notice containing -

"(1) the amount of the debt;

"(2) the name of the creditor to whom the debt is owed;

"(3) a statement that unless the consumer, within thirty days after receipt of notice, disputed the validity of the debt, or any portion thereof, the debt will be assumed to be valid by the debt collector;

211

"(4) a statement that if the consumer notifies the debt collector in writing within the thirty-day period that the debt, or any portion thereof, is disputed, the debt collector will obtain verification of the debt or a copy of a judgment against the consumer and a copy of such verification or judgement will be mailed to the consumer by the debt collector; and

"(5) a statement that, upon the consumer's written request within the thirty-day period, the debt collector will provide the consumer with the name and address of the original creditor, if different from the current creditor.

"(b) If the consumer notifies the debt collector in writing within the thirty-day period described in subsection (a) that the debt, or any portion thereof, is disputed, or that the consumer requests the name and address of the original creditor, the debt collector shall cease collection of the debt, or any disputed portion thereof, until the debt collection obtains verification of the debt or a copy of a judgment, or the name and address of the original creditor, and a copy of such verification or judgment, or name and address of the original creditor, is mailed to the consumer by the debt collector.

"(c) The failure of a consumer to dispute the validity of a debt under this section may not be construed by any court as an admission of liability by the consumer.

15 USC 1692h.

§ " **810. Multiple debts**

"If any consumer owes multiple debts and makes any single payment to any debt collector with respect to such debts, such debt collector may not apply such payment to any debt which is disputed by the consumer and, where applicable, shall apply such payment in accordance with the consumer's directions.

15 USC 1692i.

§ " **811. Legal actions by debt collectors**

"(a) Any debt collector who brings any legal action on a debt against any consumer shall-

"(1) in the case of an action to enforce an interest in real property securing the consumer's obligation, bring such action only in a judicial district or similar legal entity in which such real property is located; or

"(2) in the case of an action not described in paragraph (1), bring such action only in the judicial district or similar legal entity-

"(A) in which such consumer signed the contract sued upon; or

"(B) in which such consumer readies at the commencement of the action.

"(b) Nothing in this title shall be construed to authorize the bringing of legal actions by debt collectors.

15 USC 1692j.

§ " **812. Furnishing certain deceptive forms.**

"(a) It is unlawful to design, compile, and furnish any form knowing hat such form would be used to created the false belief in a consumer that a person other than the creditor of such consumer is participating tin the collection of or in an attempt to collect a debt such consumer allegedly owes such creditor, when in fact such person is not so participating.

"(b) Any person who violates this section shall be liable to the same extent and the same manner as a debt collector is liable under section 813 for failure to comply with a provision of this title.

15 USC 1692k.

§ **" 813. Civil Liability**

"(a) Except as otherwise provided by this section, any debt collector who fails to comply with any provision of this title with respect to any person is liable to such person in an amount equal to the sum of-

"(1) and actual damage sustained by such as a result of such failure;

"(2) (A) in the case of any action by an individual, such additional damages as the court may allow, but not exceeding $1,000; or

"(B) in the case of a class action, (i) such amount for each named plaintiff as could be recovered under subparagraph (A), and (ii) such amount as the court may allow for all other class members, without regard to a minimum individual recover, not to exceed the lesser of $500,000 or 1 per centum of the net worth of the debt collector; and

"(3) in the case of any successful action to enforce the foregoing liability, the costs of the action, together with a reasonable attorney's fees as determined by the court. On a finding by the court that an action under this section was brought in bad faith and for the purpose of harassment, the court may award to the defendant attorney's fees reasonable in relation to the work expended and costs.

"(b) In determining the amount of liability in any action under subsection (a), the court shall consider, among other relevant factors -

"(1) in any individual action under subsection (a)(2)(A), the frequency and persistence of noncompliance by the debt collector, the nature of such noncompliance, and the extent to which such noncompliance was intentional; or

"(2) in any class action under subsection (a)(2)(B), the frequency and persistence of noncompliance by the debt collector, the nature of such noncompliance, the resources of the debt collector, the number of persons adversely affected, and the extent to which the debt collector's noncompliance was intentional.

"(c) A debt collector may not be held liable in any action brought under this title if the debt collector shows by a preponderance of evidence that the violation was not intentional and resulted from a bona fide error notwithstanding the maintenance of procedures reasonable adapted to avoid any such error.

"(d) An action to enforce any liability created by this title may be brought in any appropriate United States district court without regard to the amount in controversy, or in any other court of competent jurisdiction, within one year from the date on which the violation occurs.

"(e) No provision of the section imposing any liability shall apply to any act done or omitted in good faith in conformity with any advisory opinion of the Commission, not withstanding that after such act or omission has occurred, such opinion is amended, rescinded, it determined by judicial or other authority to be invalid for any reason.

15 USC 1692l.

§ " **814. Administrative enforcement**

"(a) Compliance with this title shall be enforced by the Commission, except to the extent that enforcement of the requirements imposed under this title is specifically committed to another agency under subsection (b). For purpose of the exercise by the Commission of its functions and powers under the Federal Trade Commission Act, a violation of this title shall be deemed an unfair of deceptive act or practice in vio-

15 USC 58.

lation of that Act. All of the functions and powers of the Commission under the Federal Trade Commission Act are available to the Commission to enforce compliance by any person with this title, irrespective of whether that person is engaged in commerce or meets any other jurisdictional tests in the Federal Trade Commission Act, including the power to enforce the provisions of this title in the some manner as if the violation had been a violation of a Federal Trade Commission trade regulation rule.

"(b) Compliance with any requirement imposed under this title shall be enforced under-

15 USC 1818.

"(1) section 8 of the Federal Deposit Insurance Act, in the care of -

"(A) national banks, by the Comptroller of the Currency;

"(B) member banks of the Federal Reserve System (other than national banks), by the Federal Reserve Board; and

"(C) banks the deposits or accounts of which are insured by the Federal Deposit Insurance Corporation (other than members of the Federal Reserve System), by the Board of Directors of the Federal Deposit Insurance Corporation;

12 USC 1464.
12 USC 1730.

"(2) section 5(d) of the Home Owners Loan Act of 1933, section 407 of the National Housing Act, and sections 6(i) and 17 of the Federal Home Loan Bank Act, by the Federal Home Loan Bank Board (acting directly or through the Federal Savings and Loan Insurance Corporation), in the case of any institution subject to any of those provisions;

12 USC 1751.

"(3) the Federal Credit Union Act, by the National Credit Union Administration Board with respect to any Federal credit union;

"(4) subtitle IV of Title 49, by the Interstate Commerce Commission with respect to any common carrier subject to such subtitle;

49 USC 1301 note.

"(5) the Federal Aviation Act of 1958, by the Secretary of Transportation with respect to any air carrier or any foreign air carrier subject to that Act; and

"(6) the Packers and the Stockyards Act, 1921 (except as provided in section 406 of that Act, by the Secretary of Agriculture with respect to any activities subject to that Act.

"(c) For the purpose of the exercise by any agency referred to in subsection (b) of its powers under an Act referred to in that subsection, a violation of any requirement imposed under this title shall be deemed to be a violation of a requirement imposed under that Act. In addition to its powers under any provision of law specifically referred to in subsection (b), each of the agencies referred to in that subsection may exercise, for the purpose of enforcing compliance with any requirement imposed under this title any other authority conferred on it by law, except as provided in subsection (d).

"(d) Neither the Commission nor any other agency referred to in subsection (b) may promulgate trade regulation rules or other regulations with respect to the collection of debt collectors as defined in this title.

15 USC 1692m.

§ **"815. Reports of Congress by the Commission**
"(a) Not later than one year after the effective date of this title and at one-year intervals thereafter, the Commission shall make reports to the Congress concerning the administration of its functions under this title, including such recommendations as the Commission shall include its assessment of the extent to which compliance with this title is being achieved and a summary of the enforcement actions taken by the Commission under section 814 of the title.

"(b) In the exercise of its functions under this title, the Commissions may obtain upon request the views of any other Federal agency which exercises enforcement functions under section 814 of this title.

15 USC 1692n.

§ **"816. Relation to State Laws**
"This title does not annul, alter, or affect, or exempt any person subject to the provisions of this title from complying with the laws of any State with respect to debt collection practices, except to the extent that those laws are inconsistent with any provision of this title, and then only to the extent of the inconsistency. For purposes of this section, a State law is not inconsistent with this title if the protection such law affords any consumer is greater than the protection provided by this title.

15 USC 1692o.

§ **"817. Exemption for State regulation**
"The Commission shall by regulation exempt from the requirements of this title any class of debt collection practices within any State if the Commission determines that under the law of that State that class of debt collection practices is subject to requirements substantially similar to those imposed by this title, and that there is adequate provision for enforcement.

15 USC 1692 note.

§ **"818. Effective date**
"This title takes effect upon the expiration of six months after the date of this enactment, but section 809 shall apply only with respect to debts for which the initial attempt to collect occurs after such effective date."

Approved September 20, 1977

LEGISLATIVE HISTORY:

Public Law 95-109 [H.R. 5294]:
HOUSE REPORT No. 95-131 (Comm. on Banking, Finance, and Urban Affairs).
SENATE REPORT No. 95-382 (Comm. on Banking, Housing, and Urban Affairs).
CONGRESSIONAL RECORD, Vol. 123 (1977):

    Apr. 4, considered and passed House.

    Aug. 5, considered and passed Senate, amended.

    Sept. 8, House agreed to Senate amendment,

WEEKLY COMPILATION OF PRESIDENTIAL DOCUMENTS, Vol. 13, No. 39:

    Sept. 20, Presidential statement.

AMENDMENTS:

SECTION 621, SUBSECTIONS (b)(4) and (b)(5) were amended to transfer certain administrative enforcement responsibilities pursuant to Pub. L. 95-473, *3(b), Oct.17, 1978. 92 Stat, 166; Pub. L. 95-630, Title V. * 501, November 10, 1978, 92 Stat. 3680; Pub. L. 98-443, * 9(h), Oct. 4, 1984, 98 Stat. (708.

SECTION 803, SUBSECTION (6), defining "debt collector", was amended to repeal the attorney at law exemption at former Section (6)(F) and to redesignate Section 803(6)(G) pursuant to Pub. L. 990361, July 9, 1986, 100 Stat. 768. For legislative history, see H.R. 237, HOUSE REPORT No. 99-405 (Comm. on Banking, Finance and Urban Affairs). CONGRESSIONAL RECORD: Vol. 131 (1985): Dec.2, considered and passed House. Vol. 132 (1986): June 26, considered and passed Senate.

Appendix N

The Fair Credit Billing Act

Public Law 93-495

93rd Congress, H.R. 11221

October 28, 1974

TITLE III — FAIR CREDIT BILLING

§ 301. Short Title

This title may be cited as the "Fair Credit Billing Act".

§ 302. Declaration of purpose

The last sentence of section 102 of the Truth in Lending Act (15 USC 1601) is amended by striking out the period and inserting in lieu thereof a comma and the following: "and to protect the consumer against inaccurate and unfair credit billing and credit card practices."

§ 303. Definitions of creditor and open end credit plan

The first sentence of section 103 (f) of the Truth in Lending Act (15 USC 1602 (f) is amended to read as follows: "The term 'creditor' refers only to creditors who regularly extend, or arrange for the extension of, credit which is payable by agreement in more than four installments or for which the payment of a finance charge is or may be required, whether in connection with loans, sales of property or services, or otherwise. For the purposes of the requirements imposed under Chapter 4 and sections 127 (a) (6), 127 (a) (7), 127 (a) (8), 127 (b) (1), 127 (b) (2), 127 (b) (3), 127 (b) (9), and 127 (b) (11) of Chapter 2 of this Title, term 'creditor' shall also include card issuers whether or not the amount due is payable by agreement in more than four installments or the payment of a finance charge is or may be required, and the Board shall, by regulation, apply these requirements to such card issuers, to the extent appropriate, even though the requirements are by their terms applicable only to creditors offering open end credit plans.

§ 304. Disclosure of the fair credit billing rights

(a)Section 127 (a) of the Truth in Lending Act (15 USC 1637 (a) is amended by adding to the end thereof a new paragraph as follows:

"(8) A statement, in a form prescribed by regulations of the Board of the protection provided by sections 161 and 170 to an obligor and creditor's responsibilities under sections 162 and 170. With respect to each of two billing cycles per year, at semiannual intervals, the creditor shall transmit such statements to each obligor to whom the creditor is required to transmit a statement pursuant to section 127 (b) for such billing cycle."

"(b) Section 127 (c) of such Act (15 USC 1637 (c) is amended to read:

"(c) In the case of any existing account under an open end consumer credit plan having an outstanding balance of more than $1 at or after the close of the creditor's first full billing cycle under the plan after the effective date of subsection (a), to the extent applicable and not previously disclosed, shall be disclosed in a notice mailed or delivered to the obligor not later than the time of mailing the statement required by subsection (b)."

§ 305. Disclosure of billing contact

Section 127 (b) of the Truth in Lending Act (15 USC 1637 (b) is amended by adding at the end thereof a new paragraph as follows:

"(11) The address to be used by the creditor for the purpose of receiving billing inquiries from the obligor."

§   306. Billing practices

The Truth in Lending Act (15 USC 1601-1665) is amended by adding at the end thereof a new chapter as follows:

CHAPTER 4 - CREDIT BILLING

"Sec.
"161. Correction of billing errors.
"162. Regulation of credit reports.
"163. Length of billing period.
"164. Prompt crediting of payments.
"165. Crediting excess payments.
"166. Prompt notification of returns.
"167. Use of cash discounts.
"168. Prohibition of tie-in services.
"169. Prohibition of offsets.
"170. Rights of credit card customers.
"171. Relation to State laws

§   " 161. Correction of billing errors

"(a) If a creditor, within sixty days after having transmitted to an obligor a statement of the obligor's account in connection with an extension of consumer credit, receives at the address disclosed under section 127 (b)(11) a written notice (other than notice on a payment stub or other payment medium supplies by the creditor so stipulates with the disclosure required under section 127 (a) (8) from the obligor in which the obligor -

"(1) sets forth or otherwise enables the creditor to identify the name and account number (if any) of the obligor,

"(2) indicates the obligor's belief (to the extent applicable) that the statement contains a billing error, the creditor shall, unless the obligor has, after giving such written notice and before the expiration of the time limits herein specified, agreed that the statement was correct

"(A) not later than thirty days after the receipt of the notice, send a written acknowledgement thereof to the obligor, unless the action required in subparagraph (B) is taken within such thirty-day period, and

"(B) not later than two complete billing cycles of the creditor (in no later than ninety days) after the receipt of the notice and prior to taking any action to collect the amount, or any part thereof, indicated by the obligor under paragraph (2) either -

"(i) make appropriate corrections in the account of the obligor, including the crediting of any finance charges on amount erroneously billed, and transmit to the obligor a notification of such corrections and the creditor's explanation of any change in the amount indicated by the obligor under paragraph (2) and, if any such change is made and the obligor so requests, copies of documentary evidence of the obligor's indebtedness; or

"(ii) send a written explanation of clarification to the obligor, after having conducted an investigation, setting forth to the extent applicable the reasons why the creditor believes the account of the obligor was correctly shown in the statement and, upon request of the obligor, provide copies of documentary evidence of the obligor's indebtedness. In the case of a billing error where the obligor alleges that the creditor's billing statement reflects goods not delivered to the obligor or his designee in accordance with the agreement made at the time of the transaction, a creditor may not construe such amount to be correctly shown unless he determines that such goods were actually delivered, mailed, or otherwise sent to the obligor and provides the obligor with a statement of such determination. After complying with the provision of this subsection with respect to an alleged billing error, a creditor has no further responsibility under this section if the obligor continues to make substantially the same allegation with respect to such error.

"(b) For the purpose of the section 'billing error' consists of any of the following:

"(1) A reflection on a statement of an extension of credit which was not made to the obligor, or, if made, was not in the amount reflected on such statement.

"(2) A reflection on a statement of an extension so credit for which the obligor requests additional clarification including documentary evidence thereof.

"(3) A reflection on a statement of goods or services not accepted by the obligor or his designed or not delivered to the obligor or his designed in accordance with the agreement made at the time of a transaction.

"(4) The creditor's failure to reflect properly on a statement a payment made by the obligor or a credit issued to the obligor.

"(5)A computation error or similar error of an accounting nature of the creditor on a statement.

"(6) Any other error described in regulation of the Board.

"(c) For the purposes of this section, action to collect the amount of any part thereof, indicated by an obligor under paragraph (2) does not include the sending of statement of account to the obligor following written notice from the obligor as specified under subsection (a), if-

"(1) the obligor's account is not restricted or closed because of the failure of the obligor to pay the amount indicated under paragraph (2) of subsection (a), and

"(2) the creditor indicated the payment of such amount is not required pending the creditor's compliance with this section. Nothing in this section shall be construed to prohibit any action by a creditor to collect any amount which has not been indicated by the obligor to contain a billing error.

"(d) Pursuant to regulations of the Board, a creditor operating an open end consumer credit plan may not, prior to the sending of the written explanation or clarification required under paragraph (b) (ii), restrict or close an account with respect to which the obligor has indicated pursuant to subsection (a) that he believes such account to contain a billing error solely because of the obligor's failure to pay the amount indicated to be in error. Nothing in the subsection shall be deemed to prohibit the creditor from applying against the credit limit on the obligor's account the amount indicated to be in error.

"(e) Any creditor who fails to comply with the requirements of this section or section 162 forfeits any right to collect from the obligor the amount indicated by the obligor under paragraph (2) of subsection (a) of the section, and any finance charges thereon, except that the amount required to be forfeited under this section may not exceed $50.

§ "162. Regulation of credit reports

"(a) After receiving a notice from an obligor as provided in section 161 (a), a creditor or his agent may not directly or indirectly threaten to report to any person adversely on the obligor's credit rating or credit standing because of the obligor's failure to pay the amount indicated by the obligor under section 161 (a) (2), and such amount amy not be reported as delinquent to any third party until the creditor has met the requirements of section 161 and has allowed the obligor the same number of days (not less than ten) thereafter to make payment is provided under the credit agreement with the obligor for the payment of undisputed amounts.

"(b) If a creditor receives a further written notice from an obligor that an amount is still in dispute within the time allowed for payment under subsection (a) of the section, a creditor may not report to any third party that the amount of the obligor is delinquent because the obligor has failed to pay an amount which he has indicated under Section 161 (a) (2), unless the creditor also reports that the amount is in dispute and, at the same time, notifies the obligor of the name and address of each party to
whom the creditor is reporting information concerning the delinquency.

"(c) A creditor shall report any subsequent resolution of any delinquencies reported pursuant to subsection (b) to the parties to whom such delinquencies were initially reported.

§ " 163. Length of billing period
"(a) If an open end consumer credit plan provides a time period within which an obligor may repay any portion of the credit extended without incurring an additional finance charge, such additional finance charge may not be imposed with respect to such portion of the credit extended for the billing cycle of which such period is a part unless a statement which includes the amount upon which the finance charge for that period is based was mailed at least fourteen days prior to the date specified in the statement by which payment must be made in order to avoid imposition of that finance charge.

"(b) Subsection (a) does not apply in any case where a creditor has been prevented, delayed, or hindered in making
timely mailing or delivery of such period statements within the time period specified in such subsection because of an act of God, war, natural disaster, strike, or other excusable or justifiable cause, as determined under regulations of the Board.

§ " 164. Prompt crediting of payments
"Payments received from an obligor under an open end consumer credit plan by the creditor shall be posted promptly to the obligor's account as specified in regulations of the Board. Such regulations shall prevent a finance charge from being imposed on any obligor if the creditor has received the obligor's payment in readily identifiable form in the amount, manner, location, and time indicated by the creditor to avoid the imposition thereof.

§ " 165. Crediting excess payments
"Whenever an obligor transmits funds to a creditor in excess of the total balance due on an open end consumer credit account, the creditor shall promptly (1) upon request of the obligor refund the amount of the overpayment, or (2) credit such amount to the obligor's account.

§ " 166. Prompt notification of returns
"With respect to any sales transaction where a credit card has been used to obtain credit, where the seller is a person other than the card issuer, and where the seller accepts or allows a return of the goods or forgiveness of a debt for services which were the subject of such sale, the seller shall promptly transmit to the credit card issuer, a credit statement with respect thereto and the credit card issuer shall credit the account of the obligor for the amount of the transaction.

§ " 167. Use of cash discounts
"(a) With respect to credit cards which may be used for extensions of credit in sales transactions in which the seller is a person other than the card issuer, the card issuer may not, by contact or otherwise, prohibit any such seller from offering a discount to a cardholder to induce the cardholder to pay by cash, check, or similar means rather than use a credit card.

"(b) With respect to any sales transaction, any discount not in excess of 5 per centum offered by the seller for the purpose of inducing payment by cash, check, or other means not involving the use of a credit card shall constitute a finance charge as determined under section 106(m) if such discount is offered to all prospective buyers clearly and conspicuously in accordance with regulations of the Board.

§ " 168. Prohibition of tie-in services

"Not withstanding any agreement to the contrary, a card issuer may not require a seller, as condition to participating in a credit card plan, to open an account with or procure any other service from the card issuer or its subsidiary or agent.

§ " 169. Prohibition of offsets

"(a) A card issuer may not take any action to offset a cardholder's indebtedness arising in connection with a consumer credit transaction under the relevant credit card plan against funds of the cardholder held on deposit with the card issuer unless-

"(1) such action was previously authorized in writing by the cardholder in accordance with a credit plan whereby the cardholder agrees periodically to pay debts incurred in his open end credit account by permitting the card issuer periodically to deduct all or a portion of such debt from the cardholder's deposit account, and

"(2) such action with respect to any outstanding disputed amount not be taken by the card issuer upon request of the cardholder.

In the case of any credit card account in existence on the effective date of this section, the previous written authorization referred to in clause (1) shall not be required until the date (after such effective date) when such account is renewed, but in no case later than one year after such effective date. Such written authorization shall be deemed to exist if the card issuer has previously notified the cardholder that the use of his credit card account will subject any funds which the card issuer holds in deposit account of such cardholder to offset against any amounts due and payable on this credit card account which have not been paid in accordance with the terms of the agreement between the card issuer and the cardholder.

"(b) This section does not alter or affect the right under State law of a card issuer to attach or otherwise levy upon funds of a cardholder held on deposit with the card issuer if that remedy is constitutionally available to creditors generally.

§ " 170. Rights of credit card customers

"(a) Subject to the limitation contained in subsection (b), a card issuer who has issued a credit card to a cardholder pursuant to an open end consumer credit plan shall be subject to all claims (other than tort claims) and defenses arising out of any transaction in which the credit card is used as a method of payment or extension of credit if (1) the obligor has made a good faith attempt to obtain satisfactory resolution of a disagreement or problem relative to the transaction from the person honoring the credit card; (2) the amount of the initial transaction exceed $50; and (3) the place where the initial transaction occurred was in the same State as the mailing address previously provided by the cardholder or was within 100 miles from such address, except that the limitations set forth in clauses (2) and (3) with respect to an obligor's right to assert claims and defenses against a card issuer shall not be applicable to any transaction in which the person honoring the credit card (A) is the same person as the card issuer, (B) is controlled by the card issuer, (C) is under direct or indirect common control with the card issuer, (D) is a franchised dealer in the card issuer's products or services, or (E) had obtained the order for such transaction through a mail solicitation made by or participated in by the card issuer in which the card holder is solicited to enter into such transaction by using the credit card issued by the card issuer.

"(b) The amount of claims or defenses asserted by the cardholder may not exceed the amount of credit outstanding with respect to such transaction at the time the cardholder first notifies the card issuer of the person honoring the creed card of such claim or defense. For the purpose of determining the amount of credit outstanding in the preceding sentence, payments and credits to the cardholder's account are deemed to have been applied, in the order indicated to the payment of: (1) late charges in the order of their entry to the account; (2) finance charges in order of their entry to the account; and (3) debits to the account other than those set forth above, in the order in which each debit entry to the account was made.

§ " 171. Relation to State laws

"(a) This chapter does not annul, alter, or affect, or exempt any person subject to the provisions of this chapter from complying with, the laws of any state with respect to credit billing practices, except to the extent that those laws are inconsistent with any provision of the chapter if the Board determines that such law gives greater protection to the consumer.

"(b) The Board shall by regulation exempt from the requirements of his chapter any class of credit transactions within any State if it determines that under the law of that State that class of transactions is subject to requirements substantially similar to those imposed under this chapter or that such law gives greater protection to the consumer, and that there is adequate provision for enforcement."

§ " 307. Conforming amendments

(a) The table of chapter of the Truth in Lending Act is amended by adding immediately under item 3 the following:
"4. CREDIT BILLING..161"(b) Section 11 (d) of such Act (15 USC 1610 (d) is amended by striking out "and 130" and inserting in lieu thereof a comma and the following: "130, and 166".

(c) Section 121 (a) of such Act (15 USC 1610 (d) is amended-

(1) by striking out "and upon whom a finance charge is or may be imposed"; and

(2) be inserting "or Chapter 4" immediately after "this chapter".

(d) Section 121 (b) of such Act (15 USC 1631 (b) is amended by inserting "or Chapter 4" immediately after "this chapter".

(e) Section 122 (a) of such Act (15 USC 1632 (a) is amended by inserting "or Chapter 4" immediately after "this chapter".

(f) Section 122 (b) of such Act (15 USC 1632 (b) is amended by inserting "or Chapter 4" immediately after "this chapter".

§ " 308. Effective date

This title take effect upon the expiration of one year after the date of its enactment.

Glossary

Accounts Receivable: Term used for credit extended by any person or company to another (normally unsecured) with usual repayment terms requiring a monthly payment to amortize the balance owed.

Amortize: To liquidate or reduce an amount owed through a series of payments.

ANI: See Automatic Number Identifier.

Attorney: A legal agent authorized to appear before a court of law as a representative of a party to a legal controversy.

Automatic Number Identifier: The ability of a company to identify an 800-number caller's name and address. Every time a consumer calls one of these toll-free 800 numbers, there is a record of that call; the debt collection community frequently uses this to locate a consumer's home or business location after they have gone underground. (Use pay phones!)

Bad Debt Expense: An accounting category reserved for debts deemed uncollectible.

Bankruptcy: A legal maneuver allowing consumers or businesses to discharge all debts and liabilities. The actions of most debt collection agencies force consumers into bankruptcy instead of settling outstanding accounts.

Big Brother: Term used to describe the invasive nature of today's information society, originating from the George Orwell book *1984*. Fitting description of the feeling consumers get when dealing with the debt collection community.

Blackmail: Any payment induced by or through intimidation, by use of threats of injurious information or accusations. (A technique frequently used by unethical debt collection agencies.)

Brain damage: A state of mind common to consumers enduring difficult financial circumstances. This state of mind can intensify through frequent contacts with the debt collection industry.

Bulletproofing: Insulating yourself from financial adversaries such as creditors, debt collectors, attorneys, etc. Simple techniques include obtaining an unlisted phone number and post office box to more advanced maneuvers such as use of family trusts, corporations, etc.

Cease-Commed: Term used by the debt collection industry to describe the status of an account. When a consumer has cease-commed a debt collector this means that they have invoked federal law by sending a Cease & Desist letter via certified mail (see Appendix C), forcing the debt collector to cease collection activity of that account.

Certified Mail: Specialized postal service technique utilized to track delivery and obtain proof of delivery of letters or packages.

Chapter 7: A consumer bankruptcy filing that liquidates all non-exempt assets to pay off creditors.

Chapter 12: Bankruptcy filing reserved for working ranches, farms, etc.

Chapter 13: A type of consumer bankruptcy filing that allows the consumer to pay off creditors within a specific time period, no longer than five years. Also referred to as a "wage earner" plan.

Chapter 20: Ploy used by some bankruptcy attorneys to delay a foreclosure of real property by filing a Chapter 13 petition, then quickly converting the filing to a Chapter 7.

Charge-off: Term used by creditors to describe action taken on an uncollectible account. Alternative term used: *Written Off To Bad Debt Expense*. This action normally results in negative information lines on a credit report that can stay for at least 7 years. (Also see *uncollectible*)

Class-action lawsuit: A legal action initiated by 3 or more parties against a defendant. Many suits in this category are initiated by state or federal attorneys.

Coercion: Exercising force to obtain compliance. A favorite technique employed by debt collectors and attorneys representing creditors.

Commission: A sum or percentage paid to a person for his successful completion of services.

Consumer Credit Counseling Service (CCCS): A nonprofit organization that sells itself to the American public as the last hope for consumers buried in debt. The reality is that they are actually debt collectors for the original creditors, a fact that seems to be routinely shuffled aside and not disclosed to the consumer.

Consumer literacy test: A test proposed by the author to be given to high school students to determine competency in basic consumer skills. These skills include how to open checking and savings accounts, how to balance a checkbook, how to create/follow a budget, how credit cards work, a brief understanding of insurance, etc.

Contingency basis: A fee paid to a third party for their involvement in either a legal proceeding or debt collection. This fee is normally paid only when a successful outcome to a legal proceeding or debt has been collected, either in part or in full.

Credit grantor: Companies or individuals that extend financing to consumers. A credit grantor can be a mortgage company willing to finance a house, a bank willing to finance an automobile, or a major national credit grantor willing to extend credit through the issuance of a charge card such as Visa, MasterCard or Discover.

Credit manager: Individual that oversees the lending department in a bank, department store or other credit-granting entity. Many times this individual will work closely with the collections manager to develop collections strategies for past due/bad debts.

Credit record: National grading system filed by subject's name, birth date and social security number. Major companies providing these services include TRW, TransUnion and Equifax.

Credit repair manual: Derogatory term used by the credit reporting industry for any books that may show consumers the inside information about their industry.

Criss-cross: A directory, also known as a City Directory, that is frequently used by the debt collection community to find out information about a debtor's neighbors. One section lists households and businesses by street address; another lists all telephone numbers by exchange (in numerical order) and to whom each number is assigned. A powerful tool of information intimidation utilized to put fear into unwitting consumers.

Databases: Term used to describe the enormous pools of information managed by computers. Creditors and debt collectors will access national credit databases managed by companies like TRW, CSC/Equifax, TransUnion, etc.

Deadbeat: Term frequently used to demean consumers who are unable to pay their bills. Usually the nicest term used by the more aggressive debt collectors to upset a consumer.

Debtors' havens: Term that refers to states such as Texas and Florida which have liberal laws protecting debtors from creditors.

Deceptive forms: Another trick of the debt collector trade, these forms can take on a variety of intimidating looks—from threatening (but non-binding) documents that appear to have been issued by a court of law to demand letters that look like something issued by the IRS. Of course they're illegal . . . you don't think that will stop the debt collectors from using them, do you?

Deed in lieu of foreclosure: Technique used with mixed results by consumers unable to continue making payments on their homes. Sometimes lenders will allow debtors to deed the property back to the lender instead of suffering through the embarrassment of a foreclosure sale on the courthouse steps.

Deep discount: When a creditor sells Accounts Receivable or Bad Debts at an amount normally less than 50% of the outstanding balance. Many times these sales are made to companies that specialize in buying these types of "dead assets."

Defaulted student loans: Loan made to students to attend secondary educational institutions at low interest rates. These loans were guaranteed by the federal government as an inducement to banks to make these loans but as a result, were poorly researched before being made. Over $13 billion of these loans exist and are now owned by the U.S. government. Revised laws now enable consumers to restructure these loans. Contact the Department of Education in Washington, DC.

Deferment: Contractually agreed-to period of time a borrower is allowed to suspend payment on a debt. Usually applies to student loans and suspends the accrual of interest or late fees on the outstanding loan balance.

Deposition: Sworn statement made in the presence of a court reporter (usually) as a result of questions posed by attorneys in court (or post judgment) action. These statements are normally made outside a court of law, but are fully admissible during trial and fully binding under perjury statutes.

Discharged: To relieve of obligation, responsibility, etc. Common term used in bankruptcy court to describe the process of eliminating debtor obligations.

Discounts: Selling Accounts Receivable or Bad Debts at an amount normally in excess of 51% of the outstanding balance. Many times these sales are made to companies that specialize in buying these types of "dead assets."

Dispossession of property: Taking away property against the owner's wishes, normally as a result of non-payment.

Erroneous information: False, misleading or incorrect data. Frequently found in consumer medical or credit files across America.

Exempt assets: Assets not at risk of being seized or forfeited as a result of legal action.

Financial management: Technique used to balance income vs. expenses. Responsible financial management usually results in an excess of monies available. (This style of managing finances has yet to be mastered by the United States Government.)

Flaky loans: Questionable loans made by banks in the 1980s such as student loans or land development loans. (see *defaulted student loans*)

Fraudulent activity: Transaction designed to swindle consumers or creditors, normally cheating these groups out of goods, services or assets. (see *sign of the beast*)

Freebie report: A copy of your credit report given to you at no charge for one of two reasons . . . every consumer gets a free report from TRW just for asking and every consumer gets a free copy of their credit report if they have been declined credit.

Getting bulletproof: The process of insulating a person from lawsuits, garnishments, creditor intrusion and harassment. Popularized in Texas during the late 1980s . . . now being utilized by consumers/business people in California and the East Coast.

Golden Rule: "He who has the gold, rules." In other words, as long as you owe a creditor money, you are in a position of leverage, of negotiating strength. This leverage quickly goes away once the account has been satisfied, so use it while you can.

Greed: A motivating instinct shared by collections and credit managers that instills a desire to maximize amount of monies received. A major factor that inspires individuals to open collection agencies.

Hired gun: The hiring of third party debt collectors or attorneys to emotionally pummel a consumer in hopes of collecting an overdue account.

Hot checks: Drafts on a bank account that will be or have been returned by the bank for insufficient funds to pay face amount of check issued.

IRS refund offset program: Effort initiated by the Department of Education to recover defaulted student loans by seizing the tax refunds of consumers with the assistance of the Internal Revenue Service.

Interrogatory: Sworn statement made in writing as a result of a list of questions/inquiries by attorneys in court (or post judgment) action.

Intimidation: Inspiring or inducing fear (a favorite tactic of debt collection agencies).

Knee Breaker Collection Agency: Generic name used to describe a collection agency that may use techniques that are not endorsed by the American Collectors Association or deemed legal by the federal government under the Fair Debt Collections Practices Act. (see *Vito*)

Lawyers: (see *Attorneys*; also see *sign of the beast*)

Leverage: A negotiating position of strength; something creditors may have, debt collectors never have, and consumers almost always have.

Mail drops: Companies like Mailboxes, Etc. and others who provide a valuable service to consumers wanting to distance themselves from intrusive individuals such as debt collectors. Allows a new mailing or street address to be instantly created by consumers trying to insulate their lives.

Medical bills: The number-one reason consumers have been filing for bankruptcy, medical bills many times can be appealed or negotiated with the original provider. It is not uncommon to be grossly overcharged or mis-billed for medical services, so it's important for consumers to be aggressive when auditing these statements.

National Foundation For Consumer Credit: Parent organization for CCCS. (see *Consumer Credit Counseling Service*)

Negative information (or remarks): Statements or grades assigned on credit reports due to late payment, non-payment or default on debts owed to creditors. Bankruptcies and liens also show up under this category. Favorite point of leverage utilized by collection agencies attempting to passively blackmail consumers.

Nine-Digit Zip Code: Increasingly becoming a powerful tool for skiptracing, the 9-digit zip codes allow specific location (if a current address can be located) of a consumer, courtesy of the U.S. Post Office. (Another compelling reason to utilize post office boxes or maildrops.)

Non-dischargeable debt: Debt that cannot be eliminated through bankruptcy court. Some types of IRS debt, student loans and certain types of judgments fit into this category.

Old debt: Debt that has been charged off/written off by a creditor, normally referred to an outside "third party" collector. Old debts are usually those debts/accounts that have not had charge or payment activity for over 2 years and are the easiest to negotiate payment/removal from credit reports with creditors.

Open account: An account with a creditor that is still on the books and, in the opinion of the original creditor, collectible. These types of accounts usually are reported/updated to the credit bureaus and report late payments. They can be the most difficult to negotiate with a creditor.

Oxymoron: A term that contradicts itself, such as "jumbo shrimp" or "military intelligence" or "ethical debt collector" or "reasonable legal fees."

Paid As Agreed: Old term used on consumer credit bureau reports to describe an account that may have been renegotiated and/or settled for less than the full amount. Many creditors are now flagging these notations as negatives, so it's important that your creditor agrees to delete all information regarding a settled account, not just re-classify the account as "paid as agreed."

Paralegal: Vague title used (and abused) by many debt collectors to insinuate level of power, prestige or insight. Threats of lawsuits and jail time are frequently used by people espousing to be "paralegals."

Password: An identifying word or code that consumers may set up with the phone company and other service providers that allows only authorized individuals access to information concerning an account. Unprotected accounts are frequent targets by the debt collection community in order to obtain additional information about a consumer.

Positive identification: A means to identify without a doubt the identity of a consumer wishing to obtain a copy of their credit file. A check and balance designed to keep unauthorized people from gaining access to your information.

Postdated check: A check with a date in the future, a technique utilized to commit a person to make payment after the date written on the check. (Something a consumer should never, ever give to a debt collector.)

Profit & Loss Statement: A valuable accounting function that shows a reconciliation of all gross income and expenses to offset the same, arriving at a net profit (or loss) figure.

Prospective creditor: A credit grantor that has not yet agreed to loan/lend monies for the purchase or a home or automobile, or through the issuance of a credit card.

Public records: Another terrific source of information tapped into on a regular basis by the debt collection community in an attempt to gain insight into a debtor's activities or current location. Favorite records to be studied by the debt collectors: Divorce records, property records, tax information and motor vehicle records.

Punk: Term used to describe a debt collector who threatens consumers while safely hiding behind their telephones in an office hundreds of miles way. (see *tele-terrorists* or *unscrupulous tactics*)

Red ink: Term used to describe losses sustained by any financial entity. When individual consumers drown in red ink they may end up filing for bankruptcy; when the U.S. government engages in this financial activity it holds another treasury note or bond auction.

Regulatory agencies: Any agency empowered by either local, state or federal authorities to enforce civil laws, such as the Federal Trade Commission.

Reply card tracer: Used by Postal Service to track down return receipts that never returned to verify delivery of parcel.

Re-prioritize: The resetting of priorities in one's life, usually due to a dramatic change in circumstances. Sometimes a necessary first step toward solving one's financial problems.

Return receipts: When a letter is sent by Certified Mail, this receipt (green card for domestic mails/pink card for international) give the sender a record of who actually received/signed for letter or package sent.

Revolving charge card (or credit line): Commonly issued by major department stores and major banks, it requires a monthly payment sufficient to amortize the outstanding balance. Example: If consumers pay only the minimum balance on a $10,000 credit card and do not use the card for any additional purchases, it will take over 25 years to amortize/pay off the debt.

Risk free: A concept used in lending to describe the risk vs. return of certain types of consumer/business loans. Also refers to overdraft protection checking accounts at the House of Representatives bank in the 1980s.

Roll over: What many consumers do when dealing with credit bureaus or collection agencies, giving up without a fight. Also used to describe the apathy displayed by most Americans when asked about their input in the law making/enforcement process or budgetary responsibility of congress.

Scam: Fraudulent plan or scheme designed to separate a consumer from their money without delivering on promised goods, services (training) or value.

Scoring system: A tool used by prospective lenders to grade the credit-worthiness of a potential borrower.

/Secured creditor: Creditor whose financial position is secured by real property, such as a bank or finance company with a lien on an automobile or a mortgage company secured by the house they financed. In the event of default the secured creditor can repossess or foreclose on the property they financed, greatly reducing their chance of total loss exposure.

Secured credit card: A major national credit card (normally Visa or MasterCard) that has a credit limit secured by a cash deposit placed with the issuing bank by the cardholder. A positive recovery step for consumers who have gotten into credit problems but need a credit card in order to get a hotel room, a rental car or other business/travel- related activities.

Sign of the beast: A reference to Satan in a passage from the Revelations chapter of the Bible; also used as a derogatory term describing debt collectors and some attorneys.

Skip and skiptracing: Technique used by creditors and collection agencies to find consumers that are suddenly difficult to locate (skips). No magic here, just instant access to enormous databases containing a variety of information that, in most cases, will lead the debt collectors to your new front door.

Snake oil: A negative term used normally by an individual to discredit another. Refers to selling or promoting something that falsely claims inflated results or expectations. (A favorite term of the American Collectors Association, a trade group representing debt collectors across the U.S.)

Social security number: A nine-digit number issued by the Health and Human Services Administration to identify Americans for future social security benefits. This number has evolved into the years as a national identifier for Americans, a serial number now used for referencing credit information files, military and school records, etc.

Telephone recording device: A $20 device sold by national electronic retailer Radio Shack that allows consumers to tape telephone conversations for further review. A great equalizer when being harassed by a debt collector who thinks he's above the law.

Tele-terrorist: Term coined by this author to describe today's debt collectors who use the telephone or telefax to threaten, intimidate or coerce consumers into making (more) poor financial decisions.

Third-party debt collector: Collection agency or attorney engaged in the business of collecting debts that they did not originate. Usually taking these accounts on a contingency basis, the majority of these collection agencies work on a commission basis. The Fair Debt Collection Practices Act specifically regulates the activities of this type of collection agent.

Threats: An indication or warning of probable trouble, often illegally used by debt collectors. (see *debt collectors* or *Vito*)

Time-Value of money: A concept used by a large number of groups involved in money and finance. When relating to the debt collection business, it's an accepted fact that the longer an account goes without payment or reduced payments, the lower the chances of collecting the entire amount.

Trial by fire: Term used by individuals, often average consumers, who have acquired "street smarts" by dealing directly with their financial problems. These individuals frequently include graduates from the "school of hard knocks."

Uncollectible: Term used by creditors to describe an account that has gone past a certain period of time without payment, usually at least 6-9 months.

Underground: Another term commonly used for someone who has dropped out of sight or "skipped." Usually the result of incessant threats and phone calls from unethical debt collectors.

Unscrupulous tactics: Any number of techniques used by debt collectors in order to collect money on overdue accounts from unsuspecting consumers.

Unsecured creditor: Creditor who has no collateral covering their financial exposure. Almost all credit or charge cards fit into this category. The weakest position to be in during tough financial times, unsecured creditors are the largest employers of third-party debt collectors.

Vito: Name used to describe any individual in the debt collection industry who may use techniques that are not endorsed by the American Collectors Association or deemed legal by the federal government under the Fair Debt Collections Practices Act.

Vocational school: Non-traditional institution of higher learning designed to train students in job skills as opposed to educational degree plans in specific areas of study. Vocational schools can graduate students in 6- to 24-month course studies as opposed to 48 months in traditional colleges/university programs. This type of school is coming under increasing scrutiny by the Department of Education.

Wage-earner plan: Alternate term used to describe a Chapter 13 bankruptcy. This plan allows consumers to pay off creditors over a period not to exceed five years.

Bibliography

Abbott-Pfohl, Lillian. "City Reviews Hiring Agency To Collect On Its Tickets." *The* (Syracuse, NY) *Post-Standard*, April 25, 1994.

Abend, Jules. "Credit Matters: The Privacy Issue." *Stores Magazine*, February 1990, pp.18-19.

Barthel, Matt. "Collection Departments Lag In Automation." *American Banker*, November 18, 1993.

Bartlett, John. *Familiar Quotations*. Boston: Little, Brown, 1980.

Berner, Robert. "Debt collection company agrees to pay $200,000." *The Patriot Ledger*, December 24, 1993.

Bloom, David. "Burke, Controller Propose Centralizing Debt Collection." *Los Angeles Daily News*, July 28, 1993.

Brogan, Pamela. "Feds Charge Collection Agency With Abuses." *Gannett News Service*, August 2, 1993.

"Car-Leasing Firm Must Pay Fines." *The Boston Globe*, April 2, 1994.

Carlson, George. "Employee Has Recourse Against Bill Collector Calls." *Denver Post*, October 18, 1993.

Causey, Mike. "Docking Pay Is Now Okay." *The Washington Post*, February 13, 1994.

Cole, Jeff and Sandler, Larry. "U.S. Suit Accuses Brookfield Collection Firm Of Harassment." *The Milwaukee Sentinel*, August 3, 1993.

Collins, Chris. "Your Taxes At Work." *Gannett News Service*, June 18, 1994.

"Consumer Loan Business Pays $25,000 To Settle State's Allegations." *PR Newswire*, November 24, 1993.

"Consumers Should Claim Rights Under Law." *The Journal Record*, March 17, 1994.

Crenshaw, Albert B. "Firm Accused of Debtor Harassment." *The Washington Post*, August 3, 1993.

————. "IRS Considers Private Tax Collectors." *The Washington Post*, February 9, 1994.

Culligan, Joseph J. *You, Too, Can Find Anybody*. Miami, FL: Hallmark Press, 1993.

de Lisser, Eleena. "DAs Give Debt Collectors Competition." *The Wall Street Journal*, June 13, 1994, p. B1.

"Debt-Collection Firm Fined." *The Harrisburg Patriot*, November 25, 1993.

"Debt Collection Protection." *San Francisco Examiner*, June 1, 1993.

"Debt Collector Is Indicted." *The New York Times*, March 29, 1994.

"Debt Law May Hamper Child-Support Collection." *The Evansville (IN) Courier*, April 8, 1994.

Denenberg, Herb. "Stories Spotlight Abuses In Debt Collection." *Reading (PA) Eagle*, June 22, 1994.

Doherty, Chuck. "130 Idled As Payco Cuts Costs." *The Milwaukee Sentinel*, July 16, 1993.

Doran, Kenneth J. *Personal Bankruptcy and Debt Adjustment*. New York: Random House, 1991.

Dover, Benjamin F. *Life After Debt: The Blueprint For Surviving In America's Credit Society*. Fort Worth: Equitable Media Services, 1993.

Eggen, Dan. "Collector Of Debts Ends Career Under Duress." *The Des Monies Register*, May 12, 1993.

"Exemption Could Ease Child Support Collection." *The Las Vegas Review-Journal*, February 9, 1994.

"Federal Trade Commission, Part IV, Trade Regulations; Credit Practices, Final Rule." *Federal Register*, March 1, 1984, pp. 7740-7790.

Flores, Michele Matassa. "Repo Man Shakes Up Seattle Real Estate Market." *The Fresno Bee*, July 25, 1993.

"Foley's Agrees To Stop Debt Collection Practices." *Houston Chronicle*, May 27, 1993.

Freda, Ernie. "Federal Workers' Paychecks Easier For Creditors To Reach." *Atlanta Constitution*, February 15, 1994.

Gellene, Denise. "Bill Collectors Accused of Going Too Far." *Los Angeles Times*, August 3, 1993.

Gilgoff, Henry. "City Calls Bad Debt Collectors Very Bad." *Newsday*, June 17, 1993.

Goldstein, Arnold S. Asset Protection Secrets. Deerfield Beach, FL: *Garrett Publishing*, 1993.

Knecht, G. Bruce. "Banks Profit By Sweet-Talking Overdue Payers." *The Wall Street Journal*, June 27, 1994, p. B1.

Lewis, David. "Dialing For Debtors." *Rocky Mountain News*, November 7, 1993.

Liberante, Carrie A. "Area Debt Collection Agency Nipping Problem In Bud." *Buffalo News*, July 25, 1993.

"Loan firm settles suit with state." *Lancaster* (PA) *New Era*, December 7, 1993.

"Loan program to allow students to opt for 30-year payback." *The Dallas Morning News*, July 11, 1994, p. 2D.

"Marathon Tightens Dealer Debt Collection Policy." *US Oil Week*, May 17, 1993.

"Master Debt-Collector Proposed." *The San Diego Union-Tribune*, July 28, 1993.

McCormick, Erin. "Controller calls for war against 'deadbeats.'" *San Francisco Examiner*, July 28, 1993.

McNeil, Alex. Total Television. New York: *Penguin Books*, 1991.

"Morales Says Foley's To Change Debt Collection Practices." *The Dallas Morning News*, May 27, 1993.

"New Collection Effort Suggested." *The Des Moines Register*, January 13, 1994.

O'Steen, Van. "Act Protects Debtors From Harassment." *The Arizona Republic*, April 27, 1994.

Pankau, Edmund J. Check It Out. Houston: *Cloak & Data Press*, 1990.

"Payco Named In FTC Fair Debt Collection Practices Complaint." *Dow Jones News*, August 2, 1993.

Peterson, Susan E. "FBI Arrests 2 Credit Officers For Twin Cities Firms In Fraud Case Involving Florida Collection Agency." *The* (Minneapolis-St. Paul, MN) *Star Tribune*, May 4, 1993.

Private income tax collection proposed." *The Evansville* (IN) *Courier*, February 9, 1994.

Rothfeder, Jeffrey. *Privacy For Sale*. New York: Simon & Schuster, 1992.

"Seminar for Debt Collectors Scheduled." *The Journal Record*, March 17, 1994.

Skousen, Mark. *Complete Guide To Financial Privacy*. Alexandria, VA: Alexandria House, 1982.

"Statement of Carlton W. Fish, Director of Public Affairs, American Collectors Association, Inc. Concerning The Fair Debt Collection Practices Act." Subcommittee on Consumer Affairs & Coinage, U.S. House of Representatives, September 10, 1992.

"Statement of Elizabeth Warren, University of Pennsylvania Law School Concerning The Fair Debt Collection Practices Act." Subcommittee on Consumer Affairs & Coinage, U.S. House of Representatives, September 10, 1992.

"Statement of Dr. A. Charlene Sullivan, Associate Professor, Krannert Graduate School of Management, Purdue University Concerning The Fair Debt Collection Practices Act." Subcommittee on Consumer Affairs & Coinage, U.S. House of Representatives, September 10, 1992.

Stern, Linda. "You're Half-Covered On Collection Practices." *Reuters News Service*, August 9, 1993.

Strachman, Daniel. "Chase Unit Selects First Data System For Debt Collection." *American Banker*, March 30, 1994.

"Suit Claims Agency Defrauded Phone-Sex Line Callers." *The Harrisburg* (PA) *Evening News*, June 9, 1994.

"Sundquist Targets Deadbeat Dads." *The Commercial Appeal*, February 11, 1994.

"State Loosens Reins On Debt Collectors." *San Francisco Examiner*, June 1, 1993.

"State Sues Firm Over Debt Collection." *The Washington Times*, January 7, 1994.

"U.S. Files Suit Against Debt Collection Agency." *U.S. Newswire*, August 2, 1993.

Vogelstein, Fred. "Debt collectors busted." *Newsday*, March 24, 1994.

"A Way To Collect Power." *The Orange County Register*, August 9, 1993.

Wilcox, Ella Wheeler. Passage excerpted from "Protest." *Poems of Problems*, 1914. As quoted in the Oliver Stone film JFK, distributed by Warner Bros., 1991.

Zagaroli, Lisa. "Lawmakers Propose Changes to Ease Collections." *The Associated Press*, February 8, 1994.

Index

A

Adjusted Gross Income, 65
Air Force, 40
Alternative Payment Plans, 65, 67
American Collectors Association, 151, 230, 235, 237
American Express, v, 16, 54, 107, 108, 135, 198
AMEX, v, 108
ANI, 107, 223
Army, 40
Attorneys, vii, xiii, xvii, 2, 14, 15, 23, 24, 60, 85, 101, 128, 150, 152, 204, 224, 225, 228, 229, 230, 235
Automatic Number Identifier, 107, 223

B

Bad Check Blacklist, 43
Bad Debt Expense, 21, 138, 223, 225
Bandini, Lambert & Locke, 24
Bankcard Holders of America, 197
Bankruptcy, xiii, xix, 2, 9, 10, 11, 12, 13, 14, 15, 16, 17, 18, 27, 28, 29, 30, 51, 52, 55, 111, 137, 138, 183, 185, 197, 223, 224, 225, 228, 231, 239, 243
Banks, xvi, 5, 51, 100, 121, 156, 204, 214, 227, 229, 234
Big Brother, 30, 108, 110, 223
Book of Deuteronomy, 10
Brain damage, 3, 8, 71, 138, 224
Bulletproofing, 15, 224
Burger King, 2

C

Car payment, 133
Cash value life insurance, 11
CCCS, 49, 50, 51, 52, 151, 225, 231
Cease-Commed, 127, 225
Certified mail, xix, 35, 43, 45, 47, 70, 83, 198, 117, 152, 163, 164, 167, 169, 171, 173, 175, 179, 181, 183, 185, 187, 188, 189, 200, 224, 234
Chapter 7, xix, 2, 11, 12, 13, 14, 183, 185, 224, 225
Chapter 12, xix, 12, 14, 224
Chapter 13, xix, 2, 11, 11, 12, 13, 14, 51, 224, 225, 237
Chapter 20, xix, 21, 225
Charge off, 21
Chase Manhattan Bank, 25, 26

Chrysler, 73
Citibank, v, 73
Cleaver, June, 183, 184
Cleaver, Ward, 179, 180
Collect phone calls, 93, 211
Collection account, 21
Collect telegram fees, 93, 211
Complimentary credit report, 121
Consumer Credit Counseling Service, v, xix, 49, 52, 150, 225, 231
Consumer Fresh Start, 198
Consumer Resource Handbook, 197
Convenience users, 156
Credit report, xvi, 6, 8, 12, 13, 15, 16, 17, 21, 23, 25, 26, 41, 49, 57, 71, 90, 121, 126, 119, 133, 136, 138, 148, 149, 152, 156, 157, 158, 159, 160, 161, 162, 180, 182, 191, 192, 193, 218, 219, 225, 226, 229, 231
Credit scoring, 155
Criminal negligence, 121
Criss-cross directory, 34
Crone, Kenneth R., 26
CSC, v, 90, 186, 122, 123, 125, 144, 159, 160, 227

D

Databases, 227, 235
Debtors Anonymous, 198
Debtors' havens, 227
Deceptive forms, 100, 205, 213, 227
Deed in lieu of foreclosure, 60, 227
Deep doo-doo, 56
Department of Education, ix, 63, 64, 65, 66, 69, 70, 71, 73, 187, 188, 228, 230, 237
Discover, v, 54, 135, 198, 226
Donahue, v, 151
Drebin, Frank, 159

E

800 number, 26, 107, 123, 124, 223
Equifax, v, 2, 90, 112, 122, 123, 144, 159, 160, 226, 227

F

Fair Credit Billing Act, xx, 199, 217
Fair Credit Reporting Act, v, 123, 191, 192, 193
Fair Debt Collection Practices Act, xix, xx, 21, 22, 24, 36, 75, 101, 163, 165, 167, 169, 171, 173, 205, 206, 236

Suggested Reading

Culligan, Joseph J. *You, Too, Can Find Anybody*. Miami, FL: Hallmark Press, 1993. Provides additional insight into many of the tactics debt collectors use to find debtors.

Doran, Kenneth J. *Personal Bankruptcy and Debt Adjustment*. New York: Random House, 1991. A great reference book that lists personal exemptions state-by-state.

Dover, Benjamin F. *Life After Debt: The Blueprint For Surviving In America's Credit Society*. Fort Worth, TX: Equitable Media Services, 1993. Provides readers with a firm grasp of the credit reporting system. A must read for anyone who's already "torched" their credit report.

Goldstein, Arnold S. *Asset Protection Secrets*. Deerfield Beach, FL: Garrett Publishing, Inc., 1993. Excellent ideas on how to legally cover your assets from a qualified expert.

Pankau, Edmund J. *Check It Out*. Houston, TX: Cloak & Data Press, 1990. Additional insight into tactics the debt collectors use to find debtors.

Rothfeder, Jeffrey. *Privacy For Sale*. New York: Simon & Schuster, 1992. Bound to open your eyes . . . you'll be amazed by the amount of information that's available out there—on everyone!

Skousen, Mark. *Complete Guide To Financial Privacy*. Alexandria, VA: Alexandria House, 1982. More ideas on how to cover your assets—a nice complement to *Asset Protection Secrets* (above).

THE DOVER REPORT SURVEY

The request for current information and insights into consumer issues from our readers continues to grow, so tell us what you want to see in our upcoming newsletter! Please send this page (or a copy) to the address below.

Rate on a scale of 1-10 (with 10 being most desirable) what information is most important to you:

_____ Credit reporting issues
_____ Debt collector problems
_____ Avoiding bankruptcy
_____ Family trusts
_____ Smart banking
_____ Tax law changes and their impact
_____ Scams of the month
_____ Automobile purchase/service issues
_____ Aggressive investment opportunities
_____ Money-saving ideas
_____ Back child-support collection ideas
_____ Protection of assets
_____ Investing for retirement
_____ Consumer deal of the month
_____ Finding people
_____ Other (please specify): _____

How often would you like to see the report published?

_____ **Monthly**   _____ **Quarterly**   _____ **Bi-annually**   _____ **Annually**

Would you like the DOVER REPORT available on audiocassette?

_____ Yes   _____ No

THE DOVER REPORT SURVEY
Equitable Media Services
Post Office Box 9822-DRS/BO
Fort Worth, TX 76147-2822

Name: _____

Address: _____

City,State, Zip: _____

KNOWLEDGE IS POWER

❏**YES!** I realize that the material covered in this book can be outdated due to changes in the debt collection industry and want to be informed. Please add my name to your mailing list for any future information updates you may make available.

Name: _____

Address: _____

City/State/Zip: _____

Enclose this page (or a copy of) to:

Equitable Media Services
Post Office Box 9822-**NO BS**
Fort Worth, TX 76147-2822

or you may e-mail your name and address to Benjamin Dover at
CompuServe address: 75053,3635
Internet address: bendover@onramp.net

**Equitable Media Services maintains the highest degree of privacy at all times
and does not sell or disclose mailing list or client information to any
outside/third party.**

All correspondence is CONFIDENTIAL.

DID YOU BORROW
THIS COPY?

If so, why not get one for yourself?

Order additional copies of *__BACK OFF!__ The Definitive Guide To Stopping Collection Agency Harassment* by Benjamin F. Dover.

Please rush to me _____ copies of *__BACK OFF!__* I am enclosing **$19.00** per copy ($14.95 plus $1.16 tax and $2.89 postage/handling).

Name: _____

Address: _____

City, State, Zip: _____

Enclose this page (or a copy of) with your check or money order and mail to:

BACK OFF!
Equitable Media Services
Post Office Box 9822-**GET 'EM!**
Fort Worth, TX 76147-2822

❏ **YES!** Please add to me to your mailing list for all future updates.

Equitable Media Services maintains the highest degree of privacy at all times and does not sell or disclose mailing list or client information to any outside/third party.

If you are interested in obtaining quantity discounts, please write to the address above for additional information.

All orders and correspondence are CONFIDENTIAL.

250

Did You Know....

- A $3 shampoo purchase will save you up to $150 off airfares within the 48 states & Canada?
- You can stay at over 70 Holiday Inns at 50% OFF?
- When flying to over 80 major U.S. cities, a friend can travel with you for free?
- College students can fly coast to coast or to 80 other U. S. destinations for only $179 round trip?
- You can take a companion to over 100 U. S. cities for only $149?

You can be in the "*know*" with Benjamin Dover's Smart Consumer Insider Travel Secrets Newsletter.

Every issue of the Insider Travel Secrets Newsletter gives you the *inside* track each month on the *hottest* money saving travel tips & promotions available!

Plus! Save `15 Off the base subscription rate if you order now, only `2.25 an issue!

- -

YES! I want to *know* with Benjamin Dover's Smart Consumer Insider Travel Secrets!

1 year subscription	$42
Special Offer	- $15
Your price	*Only* $27

Check Payment method

___Check/Money Order ___VISA

___MasterCard ___American Express

Name:_____

Address:_____

City/State/Zip:_____

Home Phone:_____ Work Phone:_____

Card #_____

Exp. Date:_____ Signature:_____

Mail this form and your payment to:
BFDover's Insider Travel Secrets
P.O Box 9822 • Ft. Worth, TX 76147-2822